Toward the Better Country

Toward the Better Country

Church Closure and Resurrection

L. GAIL IRWIN

FOREWORD BY DAVID SCHOEN

RESOURCE *Publications* · Eugene, Oregon

TOWARD THE BETTER COUNTRY
Church Closure and Resurrection

Resource Publications
An Imprint of Wipf and Stock Publishers
199 W. 8th Ave., Suite 3
Eugene, OR 97401
www.wipfandstock.com

ISBN 13: 978-1-62564-231-8
Manufactured in the U.S.A.

Scripture quotations, unless otherwise noted, are from the New Revised Standard Version of the Bible, © 1989 by the Division of Christian Education of the National Council of Churches of Christ in the United States of America and are used by permission.

The poem "Cargo" is reprinted from *Cargo,* by Greg Kimura; copyright © 2012

For My Father

CARGO

You enter life a ship laden with meaning, purpose and gifts
sent to be delivered to a hungry world.
And as much as the world needs your cargo,
you need to give it away.
Everything depends on this.

But the world forgets its needs,
and you forget your mission,
and the ancestral maps used to guide you
have become faded scrawls on the parchment of dead Pharaohs.
The cargo weighs you heavy the longer it is held
and spoilage becomes a risk.
The ship sputters from port to port and at each you ask:
"Is this the way?"
But the way cannot be found without knowing the cargo,
and the cargo cannot be known without recognizing there is a way,
and it is simply this:
You have gifts.
The world needs your gifts.
You must deliver them.

The world may not know it is starving,
but the hungry know,
and they will find you
when you discover your cargo
and start to give it away.

—Greg Kimura

Contents

Foreword   *ix*

Acknowledgments   *xi*

1   Introduction   1

2   The Rise and Fall of Sacred Places   10

3   Expressions of Grief in the Faith Community   23

4   Discerning the Failure to Thrive: Lay Leaders   40

5   Discerning the Failure to Thrive: Pastors   57

6   Discerning the Failure to Thrive: Regional Pastors   73

7   Multiple Paths to the Future   84

8   A Tale of Two Closures   104

9   Laying the Foundation for Future Ministry   123

10   Seven Ways to Say Goodbye   133

11   New Wine for New Wineskins   150

*Appendix A: Guidelines for Congregations Considering Merger
    with One or More Congregations and That Seek the Financial
    Support of the Presbytery of Milwaukee*   159

Appendix B: Winnebago Presbytery   163

*Appendix C: Services from the Massachusetts Conference, U.C.C.
    for Member Churches considering closure*   168

Additional Resources   172

Bibliography   177

Foreword

"Do you have resources for closing or selling a church as well as discerning how or if to continue as a congregation without a worship place? The congregation I serve would like to close as gracefully as possible and we are open to the wisdom of others who have traveled the road before."

EACH WEEK, MY OFFICE receives e-mails like this from pastors and congregations facing difficult decisions about the future of their churches and ministries, whether a congregation needs to sell its building, merge with another congregation, or bring an end to its life. There is an increase in the number of congregations facing such conversations and decisions throughout denominations and our nation. There are also many congregations that are avoiding the conversation.

There are many reasons why congregations close. Perhaps the most basic is simply that the average lifespan of congregations compares to the average lifespan of an individual. Congregations that make it through the initial years of a new church development have an average lifespan of 70 to 100 years. With the many congregations started as new churches in the 1950s and 60s, there is the likelihood that we will see an increase in churches closing. Many are made up of aging members who have participated in their churches since their early years.

Few of us who grew up in the church in the 50s and 60s could have imagined in those years that there would be such a decline in church participation and in congregation viability as there is now. Those of us ordained during the 1970s could hardly have foreseen the challenges that now confront our ministries in local congregations and denominations. The fastest growing religious population today is "nones"—those folks who have no religious affiliation. New generations, although spiritual, missional, and civic-minded, do not seek to participate in the traditional church. The decline throughout the church, locally, regionally, and nationally, casts a pall of grief over our systems when we see the ministries that we have nurtured through the years collapse despite our best efforts.

Toward the Better Country: Church Closure and Resurrection is a helpful book for all settings of the church, not only for its honest and practical advice but also for its theological depth, which encourages readers to see the current situation of church closure in the light of God's resurrection power, creating new realities and futures even (and especially) in the midst of death. Gail Irwin helps us to affirm that God has a future for the church and its mission for those who have eyes to see and ears to hear the new thing that God is doing through challenging times and difficult decisions. Irwin, who experienced the difficulty of closing a congregation, calls us to hope and confidence in God to reshape the church for a new time. Of course, in order for something new to begin, God calls us to let go of that which has already been.

Letting go of that which has been is not easy for congregations, or regional and national ministries. *Toward the Better Country: Church Closure and Resurrection* has useful information and reflections on church closure for all settings of the church. Irwin gives honest, direct advice to help congregations let go and face the closing of their ministry and fellowship, trusting that in doing so God is able to make a future possible that human intent could not. Each chapter closes with engaging Biblical texts and reflection questions for churches to use as they discern the movement of God's Spirit and their faithful response to the question: "How well can we live for the time we have been given by God?"

Congregations and pastors, like the one that wrote the e-mail quoted above, are looking for resources on how their churches can live and die "as gracefully (and faithfully) as possible." They are looking for "the wisdom of others who have traveled the road before." It is good to know that now when I receive such e-mails, I have this valuable resource book to recommend to congregations and pastors. Irwin shares her own experience and provides good research, helpful insights, and a faithful witness to the God who is leading us ever closer to the promised realm and future.

Reverend David C. Schoen
Congregational Assessment, Support and Advancement Team Leader
Local Church Ministries, United Church of Christ

Acknowledgments

THE PROCESS OF RESEARCHING and writing this book has been a huge honor for me, and I am deeply grateful to everyone who has offered me wisdom and guidance in completing it.

I wish to thank the members of the former Preble Park Presbyterian Church for their commitment to create a faith community that was welcoming of all. I thank God for allowing me to be part of that ministry for a portion of their fifty-year lifespan, and for the rich education I received in the company of the saints there.

The project was conceived in the office of the Rev. Amy Bertchausen, executive director of the Samaritan Counseling Center in Menasha, Wisconsin, whose gentle insights inspired me to learn more about the hearts of struggling churches. The Rev. David Moyer, Wisconsin Conference UCC minister, posed thoughtful questions that helped me shape a project that would be useful to church leaders.

I am grateful to the Louisville Institute for entrusting me with a Pastoral Study Project grant that allowed me the time and resources needed to be physically present for interviews with church leaders around the upper Midwest.

Several trusted advisors assisted me in the formation of the manuscript. They include the Rev. Linda Kuhn, of Sandbur Consulting, who helped me stay attentive to the guidance of the Holy Spirit. Dr. Michael Lukens, stated clerk of the Winnebago Presbytery (PCUSA), brought wisdom in the areas of history, polity, and church law. Janet Puhlmann brought a heart both broken and mended by her deep love for churches that have closed. Ellie Wilson provided much needed editorial assistance. Anne Simpson was a constant source of encouragement and support. And the entire staff of the Falls Family Restaurant provided generous hospitality and many poached eggs during the writing process.

My husband Charles dared to say "Yes" to this project before he knew what he was saying yes to. And my daughter Evelyn accompanied me to visit many churches, helping me see them through the next generation's eyes.

Most of all, I am grateful to the dozens of lay leaders, clergy, and regional pastors who inspired me by sharing their stories of grief, discernment, experimentation, and resurrection. Some were told in formal interviews and others whispered in church hallways. Many were accompanied by prayers, laughter, and tears. In most cases, I have chosen not to reveal the names of these storytellers or their churches, in order to preserve the confidence they placed in me. But each of them is named in God's heart.

To all those faithful leaders who have seen a congregation through a closure or significant change, thank you for renewing my hope in the future of Christ's church. This book is your story, and I pray that its telling will offer courage and creativity to church leaders who imagine a *better country*, and are not afraid to pursue it.

1

Introduction

From one person, and this one as good as dead, descendants were born,
"as many as the stars of heaven and as the innumerable grains of sand
by the seashore."

All of these died in faith without having received the promises, but
from a distance they saw and greeted them. They confessed that they
were strangers and foreigners on the earth, for people who speak in this
way make it clear that they are seeking a homeland. If they had been
thinking of the land that they had left behind, they would have had
opportunity to return. But as it is, they desire a better country, that is,
a heavenly one. Therefore God is not ashamed to be called their God;
indeed, he has prepared a city for them.

HEBREWS 11: 12–16

MY CHURCH'S STORY

I GREW UP IN the heyday of the mainline church, in a growing suburb of
Los Angeles, among nuclear families living in the burgeoning subdivisions
that replaced the avocado orchards of an earlier time. My church was a
product of the new era. Started in 1960, my parents were charter members.

The United Church of Christ was a young denomination, and the church attracted mobile, upper-middle-class Christians moving to California, who populated its sprawling Sunday School wing and married in its romantic contemporary sanctuary. I remember busy classrooms that smelled of paste, crowded Christmas programs, and youth group meetings attended by dozens of students.

When I entered seminary in the mid 1980s, I presumed the church I was devoting my life to would be similar to the one I grew up in. But by the time I was ordained a few years later, I felt the culture shifting in ways I could not predict. I moved to the Midwest and accepted a call to a small-town congregation where I did everything I was taught to do: taught confirmation class to teenagers, married young couples, and buried the dead. The church didn't grow, but it held its own as the elderly passed away and new families moved in. Reading the news and feeling the pulse of culture, I had the sense that change was on the horizon, but in that small town, the cyclone of history didn't touch down very often. I immersed myself in the daily routines of ministry, and I loved it.

About a decade later, at the turn of a new century, I asked God for a new challenge. God obliged and sent me to a small, urban church that was on the brink of collapse. Started in 1960, like my home church, its founders had high hopes for it to grow into a large, suburban "program church." Based on the history of American churches up to that time, this wasn't a far-fetched dream. But for many reasons, that dream did not take hold. The suburban housing developments that sprang up in the area put this church off the high-traffic roadways. The pastors chosen were perhaps not equipped with the skills needed to grow the church after its initial burst of energy. The congregation had no partners in its denominational family to offer support; instead, it was seen by neighbor churches as competition.

In the early 1980s, when the church had reached its peak of about 175 members, they called in a consultant who advised them to leave their location and purchase land for a building more visible from a major highway. Instead, they built an addition, including a larger sanctuary and office space.

With the new addition built but not yet paid for, the church began to spiral into decline. A previous pastor was accused of sexual misconduct. Another was blamed for poor handling of the accusation. In the mounting tension, members jumped ship, leaving the small church saddled with betrayal and debt.

When I arrived at this church as their pastor, they were depressed and listless. Their membership had plummeted, and there were about forty worshipers each week, barely enough to pay my half-time salary, manage the building, and provide basic programming. But when the option of closing surfaced in conversation, it was not seriously considered. That would amount to giving up.

Despite their hard times, the church had a number of unusual assets. The leadership included several young retirees, local artists, and musicians who were passionate about the ministry. The congregation had effectively reached out to gay and lesbian Christians in the community and was known informally as a welcoming place for all. It was embedded in a neighborhood that was now more urban than suburban, a community experiencing ethnic and demographic change.

I spent several years rebuilding what I imagined was a functional faith community. Position descriptions were clarified for leaders. We paid off the mortgage. The Sunday School was revived and strengthened. I attended revitalization conferences held by my denomination. Spiritual formation became a new focus for us. A few new members joined. We shared our building with a Hmong congregation, a food cooperative, a drumming group, and an AA meeting. We "came out of the closet" as a church welcoming of gay and lesbian Christians. Although progress was slow, it seemed to be steady.

Then, about seven years into my tenure, worship attendance began to drop. For a struggling church like mine, such a sign was like the slowing of a heartbeat. Still, I was not willing to give up. Finally, I asked for a sabbatical. I wanted to explore what it might mean to do church in new ways. I went away for three months, studied the emergent church movement, and came back full of ideas.

When I returned, it was September, 2008, the month that insurance giant AIG collapsed and the stock market came down with it. Almost immediately, I could see the church was sick. It was like returning home to find a familiar parent aging in unfamiliar ways. My little congregation was showing all the signs of impending death. They turned inward and communicated in hushed tones. Committees began to function outside their normal boundaries. Programs were planned, but no one would show up. When I tried to get people to talk about what they were experiencing, they were silent.

Less than a year after my return from sabbatical, I was asked to resign. I had been with them eleven years. I had failed to help them revitalize, and now I was leaving without helping them close.

Throughout my tenure in that congregation, I sought professional and pastoral advice on how to love and pastor them through decline. Instead, I received a lot of advice about revitalization and church growth. But this was a congregation that had lost its capacity to grow. I knew I was "beating a dead horse." What no one helped me with was how to lay the horse peacefully to rest.

This book is the outcome of my experience with that congregation, and the compilation of dozens of interviews I have conducted since then with lay people, clergy, and denominational leaders who have experienced the decline and death of churches. I have found God's presence in the telling and hearing of stories like these, and I hope you will too. My goal is to help you reflect on what your church and denomination are experiencing in the day-to-day process of leading declining congregations. My intention is not just to help churches close with dignity, but to help them be resurrected as part of the universal church, in new forms that address people's continuing spiritual longings, our hunger for justice and peace, and our culture's need for places of social engagement.

YOUR CHURCH'S STORY

If you have opened this book, you probably have already observed that the pews at your church are not as full as they used to be on Sunday morning. In fact, I'm guessing that you have already spent significant energy on keeping your church open. You have spearheaded stewardship programs, walked the neighborhood with flyers, launched fundraisers and capital campaigns, or streamlined your church's organizational structure. You are one of the first to arrive at a church function, and one of the last left folding up the chairs. Sometimes, you are the only one who shows up.

You have gone to many conferences and workshops, and you have the tote bags and binders to prove it. You came home with lots of new ideas, but somehow they are all a blur now. You have sat through denominational meetings listening to other church leaders talk about their meaningful mission projects, youth outings, and building additions. Sometimes you have wished you could disappear under the table when it came your turn to tell about something exciting your church is doing. On your keychain, you carry keys to the church's front door, the Sunday School supply closet, and the tool shed, but there is one door you haven't been able to unlock: the one that leads to your church's survival.

Many committed Christians will do whatever it takes to keep their churches open when faced with a decline in membership, financial resources, or spiritual energy. We do these things because we love our churches and are wired as Christians to maintain them for our beloved elderly, ourselves, and our children. But history has shown that no local church is meant to live forever in its present form. Like people, churches are born, live and breathe, fulfill their missions, and pass away. But because the church is God's project, your declining church may also be the seedbed of some new ministry venture God is dreaming of.

If you or your congregation needs to have a conversation about significant decline and the possible options available to you in the future, including downsizing for sustainability, merger, partnership with another organization, or closure, this book is a tool to assist in that dialog. You have come to the right place.

OUR CHURCH'S STORY

The fact that you are reading this book is an indication that you are facing the reality of your church's present and future health in a positive way. More and more, church leaders are looking seriously at the financial and emotional cost of maintaining declining structures and seeking creative solutions.

But there are some congregations that refuse to take action and keep relying on old remedies for a new condition. Seeing their numbers decline, they advertise more, or bring in bigger balloons for Rally Day to attract young families. Churches like my former congregation have even built additions and hoped that "if we build it, they will come." But our former assumptions about what once made a church successful do not necessarily apply anymore.

The twentieth-century institutional church, with its emphasis on membership loyalty and continuity across generations of families, is quickly becoming extinct in a culture of high mobility and cautious commitment. Many Christians sense that the church is entering a time of re-evaluation and rebirth: we are being called back to a more "missional"[1] model, an organization focused not on its own institutional life, but on its unique mission to serve others in the manner of Christ. The mission may be enacted with

1. For a brief description of the concept of a missional church, see Bullard, "Mission Banality Revisited."

or without buildings, paid pastors, or the traditional array of programming options offered by the twentieth-century church. It will thrive as the church always has: by the Word of life and the Spirit's guidance.

The church that we and our parents grew up in was a model that yielded great progress for Christ. Every church in every small town or city had the potential to extend Christ's mission. These were places of social engagement, where all ages could learn about the Bible and the daily practice of compassion, hear stories about the mission of the church in Africa, roll bandages for soldiers during a war, enjoy Bible studies and potlucks, care for grieving widows, and learn to speak the language of their new, adopted nation. The institutional church of the nineteenth and twentieth centuries was a model that deserves respect for all that it accomplished. In many places, this model will continue to be an effective way to grow Christians for years to come.

But Christ is not finished with us yet! The decline of old models of the church is a sign that we are being reshaped to foster deeper discipleship among a more committed core of Christ's followers. As the writer of Hebrews reminds us, our ancestors in the faith pursued "the better country" without ever arriving there. That better country is still ahead of us.

As you navigate your concerns about your church's survival, you need to know that you are not alone, your church's decline is not your fault, and your church is not a "failure." The decline of your church is part of a larger cultural shift that is changing the place of the church in society. My church and yours are just small dots on that landscape.

THE STORY OF THIS BOOK

This book is the compilation of over thirty interviews with lay leaders, pastors, and regional leaders who told me about their personal experience with nearly forty struggling churches from eight denominations. Their stories are woven in with my own experience as a small church pastor. They will hopefully help you begin the kind of honest conversations, spiritual reflection, and concrete planning that accompany a major change in your ministry, whether God leads you toward a transformation of your current ministry, partnership with another congregation, or closure and resettlement in new churches.

Because so many churches have opened, flourished, receded, and closed throughout history, we will begin with stories of why churches have always been closing. You will learn that church decline is not all your fault. Your church's members are not lazier or less generous than those at other churches. It's not that you haven't worked hard enough. It's not all your pastor's fault. While there are some things individuals and leaders can do to hasten the decline of churches, the causes are complex and come from both within and outside the congregation. You will learn that your church is not a failure if it is small and financially unsustainable. It is not a failure if it chooses to sell its building, function without a pastor, or close its doors and disperse its membership to other churches.

However, congregations that refuse to face the grief and change required in this era of decline may make their situations worse by preventing healthy adaptation. The tasks and responsibilities of laity, clergy, and regional leaders in a church's discernment process will be addressed.

In the central chapters of the book, you will hear stories from churches that have closed or radically altered their ministry in the recent past, why and how they did so, and what their members are accomplishing in mission today. In most cases, these congregations dealt with their collective grief and creatively addressed the changes needed to carry on with ministry in a new way.

In the final chapters of the book, you will hear of concrete ways that ministry not only survives, but thrives, among people of faith who courageously face the future with hearts open to the new thing God is doing in our midst every day. Your congregation can faithfully address your grief and pass your spiritual and material legacies on to the future. You can do great ministry in new ways when you find the courage to let go of older forms that are binding you to the past.

When I first began collecting the stories shared here, I was deep in the grief of my own church's closure. But the more I learned from others who have walked this road, the more I found hope in the ways God is leading us to into the future. Human creativity is merging with God's ingenuity to bring more people into an encounter with Christ. There are new forms of church being created by God's creative hand in the wake of current church decline, and they are risky and inspiring and fun!

As you read, take courage in the fact that you are among a generation of Christians who are living on the threshold of a new time. *God chose us for this time!* We are the ones who must faithfully dismantle some of the beloved old forms that gave life to God's Word in the past. We are being led to love God's mission more than any church building or institutional form we have ever known. The legacy we inherited: those beautiful old edifices—the studious, educated clergy, the culture in which church was at the center of our social lives—these may not be the legacies we pass on. But we have a chance to pass on something even better: a more focused engagement in discipleship, a pioneering spirit for seeing what has not yet been seen and pursuing it: *the better country*, the heavenly one.

In my experience with a church in decline, I learned to say "This is God's project." This was not to negate my responsibility in leading the church, but it was a reminder that we are not in complete control of the outcomes of our labor, nor do we get to see God's "finished product" in our lifetimes. I come to this endeavor with the belief that a faithful reshaping, merger, or closure may be more in keeping with God's will than a strenuous effort to stay open at all costs.

Regardless of the shape our churches take in the future, God's project will go on.

REFLECTION

Lord, you have been our dwelling place
in all generations.
Before the mountains were brought forth,
or ever you had formed the earth and the world,
from everlasting to everlasting you are God.
You turn us back to dust,
and say, "Turn back, you mortals."
For a thousand years in your sight
are like yesterday when it is past,
or like a watch in the night.

PSALM 90:1–4 (NRSV)

- With a partner or group, name some of the circumstances that have changed in your community and your church's ministry in the last 5 to 10 years.

- List some ways your congregation has responded to these changes in the recent past. Where have you sensed God opening doors, and where have you encountered dead ends?

- What would you like to ask or say to God about the changing circumstances in your ministry setting?

2

The Rise and Fall of Sacred Places

Come to him, a living stone, though rejected by mortals yet chosen and precious in God's sight, and like living stones, let yourselves be built into a spiritual house, to be a holy priesthood, to offer spiritual sacrifices acceptable to God through Jesus Christ. For it stands in scripture:

"See, I am laying in Zion a stone,
a cornerstone chosen and precious;
and whoever believes in him will not be put to shame."

I PETER 2:4–5 (NRSV)

WHEN I WAS ELEVEN years old, my parents took us on a vacation to Europe. One day we toured the Scottish countryside and visited the ruins of several ancient castles and abbeys built in the medieval period.

As an adolescent, I knew nothing about the history of the abbeys, or of the Christian conquest of Britain. All I knew that day was that I loved ancient ruins. It had snowed lightly, and by the time we got to one particular abbey, there was a soft, white dust covering everything.

At first, I was perplexed by my parents' choice of such a vacuous place to visit. Nobody was there except our family of six. There was no gift shop, no snack bar, and no tour guide. If there were historical plaques, I paid no attention to them. There were only the tracings of the original walls that made up the complex, and a portion of a grand sanctuary, with its lacelike windows still proudly erect.

I made footprints in the thin snow and explored the fallen stone structure. It was clear how grand the whole edifice had once been. It was so quiet that the holy place had driven even my noisy siblings into silent reverie.

For a moment, I stood alone in an open area that must have once been a large hall, but that was now just a meadow surrounded by a low stone border. And then a feeling washed over me: I was standing in an important place and time, as if I was meant to be here, as if I was welcomed. With years of hindsight, I would call it an experience of the Holy Spirit. Whatever it was, it moved my tiny, adolescent heart, and I never forgot it.

I have since learned a little more about the tumultuous history of the Scottish abbeys. Like the California missions whose shadow I grew up in, they were built from both religious fervor and political aspirations. They must have been an imposing site, their grand buttresses rising up out of the foggy, green Scottish hills, their filigree windows, state-of-the-art plumbing systems, and bustling agricultural economies.

Melrose Abbey, one of the most well-known abbey ruins in Scotland, occupies a site that housed a monastic community as far back as the seventh century. It later became a thriving religious and agricultural center that lasted four hundred years, although it was repeatedly attacked in territorial skirmishes.[1] Its most fervent protector was Robert the Bruce, the last of the Scottish kings, who defended it against the British until his death in 1329. When he died, he requested that his heart be buried in its foundation as a sign of his loyalty to his territory and people.[2] But as the Brits and Scots battled over territory, Melrose suffered more battle scars, and ultimately, all its salvageable building materials were carried off by the locals.

Abbeys like Melrose fostered the faith of many Christians. They were centers for education, civilization, prayer, and political power. They were the sites of many battles, of literal and figurative blood-letting. Their ruins stand as a testament to another time, a realm run by ecclesiastical power and political coercion.

But certainly, the abbeys were also vessels of spiritual energy. Some of their ruins have been identified by Celtic Christians as "thin places." A thin place is one where generations of Christians have sensed an "opening" between heaven and earth, a physical place where the Spirit breaks through

1. Lonie, "The History of Melrose."
2. Lonie, "Melrose Abbey and the Heart of the Bruce," para. 41.

and can be perceived by the faithful. Perhaps the abbey I visited had been permeated with spiritual energy that did not dissipate when it fell into ruins. This may sound like superstitious hogwash, but anyone who has made a pilgrimage to a holy place, whether it be an ancient cathedral or the grave site of a loved one, knows the holiness inherent in sacred places.

Such places remind us that we are not alone in our concern for the rise and fall of churches. There exists before us a long parade of faithful people who invested blood, sweat, and tears in the building of faith communities they had high hopes for, only to see them corrupted, politicized, battled over, neglected and abandoned, torn down and rebuilt over the centuries. We are not the first Christians to bury our hearts in the foundation of sacred places.

I have stood in many holy places throughout my life where I felt the heartbeats of the faithful who had walked there before. While I believe the Holy Spirit exists in these places, even when they are no longer functioning churches, I also believe the Spirit moves with us into new places where new ministry springs up. While the ruins of churches dot the globe, the Spirit of Christ refuses to be disembodied.

WHERE DID EVERYONE GO?

Although the Spirit continues to live in both ancient ruins and current churches, the *people* seem to be increasingly absent. For the past 75 years, Gallup has conducted an annual poll asking Americans the same basic question: *Have you attended worship in the past week?* And every year, for the last 75 years, the answer "yes" has been uttered by about 40 percent of the population.[3] This is a comforting but confusing statistic for those of us attending mainline churches who notice the empty pews around us. If the people aren't in our churches, where are all they all going?

For a couple decades, many of us assumed they were transferring their membership to evangelical churches or the new "mega-churches" that flourished in the 90s. To a certain extent, that was true. Large, evangelical churches experienced a boom of growth in the 90s. But by the turn of the new century, even large churches were beginning to see declining participation. In 2010, the Crystal Cathedral, a pioneering mega-church in Orange County, California, filed for bankruptcy.[4] Other mega-churches around the

3. Newport, "Americans' Church Attendance Inches Up," para. 1.
4. Santa Cruz, "O.C. Catholic Diocese to Buy Bankrupt Crystal Cathedral," para. 2.

country have found themselves laying off staff members as they respond to economic pressure caused by the recession that began in 2008.[5]

It turns out that asking Americans about their behavior is not always the best way to find out what they are actually doing. Episcopal church researcher Kirk Hadaway found significantly different results when he estimated the actual number of churches that exist (a number that is not officially documented anywhere) and the corresponding average attendance in each, as reported by their denominational structures. Using these calculations, he concluded that about 20.4 percent of Americans have attended church in the last week, about half that reported in the Gallup poll.[6]

Taken individually, few denominations have escaped numerical decline and the loss of churches. The United Methodist Church has lost about 20 percent of its churches since 1967.[7] The United Church of Christ (UCC), which counted 6,900 churches in 1962, reported 5,100 churches in 2011, a 25 percent loss. This number becomes more alarming when coupled with total membership numbers in the UCC, which have dropped by 47 percent in the same period.[8]

In the year 2009 alone, the Presbyterian Church USA lost roughly 3 percent of its membership from the previous year. The Rev. Gradye Parsons, Stated Clerk of the General Assembly, said, "What continues to sadden me is that the overwhelming majority of the loss in membership is in the category of 'other,' which means these are brothers and sisters in Christ who did not die or transfer to another congregation, but probably quietly slipped out the back door."[9]

While a few denominations are growing modestly, including the Church of Jesus Christ of Latter-Day Saints, the Assemblies of God, and the Jehovah's Witnesses, other churches that have previously weathered the storm of decline, like the Southern Baptists and Roman Catholics, are now experiencing losses, too.[10] "The challenge to Christianity in the U.S. does not come from other religions but rather from a rejection of all forms of

5. Light, "Joblessness Hits the Pulpit," para. 5.
6. Smietana, "Statistical Illusion," para. 4.
7. Association of Religious Data Archives.
8. Ibid., and 2011 Annual Report, United Church of Christ.
9. Youngs, "Stated Clerk Releases PC(USA) 2009 Statistics," para. 6.
10. Jenks, "National Council of Churches 2009 Yearbook."

organized religion," says a report of the American Religious Identification Survey of 2009.[11]

The result of these losses is that a growing number of churches now lack "critical mass": the number of people necessary to sustain their institutional life for more than a few years into the future. A few existing churches in decline may find a recipe for regrowth and increase their membership again. Some of them will find new ways to do ministry on a smaller scale. Others will sell their buildings and merge with neighboring congregations or disperse altogether.

IS IT US OR IS IT THEM?

Why has this dramatic loss in church attendance occurred? I have sat in on many meetings of lay people who fretted about former members and their lack of commitment to the church. "If they would just come back, everything would be fine again," they suggest. I have also listened in on church leaders who indict the church itself for its flabby faith convictions and "mission drift." Some feel that institutional conflict and loss of purpose have caused people to drift away from the church. What is the true cause of church decline? Let's consider some possible answers to this question.

The Ebb and Flow of History

Church growth and decline in the United States has had its own ebb and flow over history. If we are tempted to think that church closure is a new phenomenon, the record refutes this.

Keith[12] is a denominational leader whose region includes parts of three states and several small cities. When I asked him about his experience with church closure, he put the issue in perspective by reading me the statistics on closures in his region going back to the mid-nineteenth century. Over a period of 160 years, his district had seen 213 churches opened that were closed by the early 1970s. Church closure is not a new phenomenon. Cultural change and migration have impacted churches in every period of history.

Sociologist Robert Wuthnow and journalist Amy Frykholm argue that while "voluntary church membership has been strong in American history,

---

11. Kosmin and Keysar, "American Religion Identification Survey," 2.

12. Interviewee and church names are pseudonyms, except where surnames are used.

it has never been stable." Church membership and attendance have "waxed and waned over the years." Frykholm identifies two periods of growth, one being the mid-nineteenth-century's Second Great Awakening period. During this time, frontier preachers, many of them Baptist and Methodist, held revivals and built small congregations that emphasized the personal commitment of believers. A hundred years later, the post–World War II era was a time of population and economic growth when the church experienced what Frykholm calls "a dynamic religious marketplace," in which the church became "a primary means of social belonging."[13]

It was in the wake of this second wave of growth that many of today's older adults were raised in the church. The church of the 1950s and 1960s is still our "normal." Yet, the cultural conditions of that period no longer exist. The U.S. today is more ethnically and religiously diverse than it was a half-century ago. More women work outside the home (from 34 percent in 1950 to 60 percent in 2000),[14] and families are configured in less "traditional" forms than they were fifty years ago, with 35 percent of children living with a single parent.[15] All these factors affect people's ability to stay socially engaged.

Robert Putnam, in his book *Bowling Alone,* documented the decline in Americans' interest in collective pursuits such as churches, clubs, and team athletics and the effect this has had on our ability as a culture to build healthy connections for socialization, commerce, and the common good, something Putnam refers to as "social capital."[16] Layer on all of this the economic downturn that began in 2008, and we can understand why local churches are experiencing lower attendance and, in some cases, closing their doors. We are only one of many social institutions that have seen this type of decline. And these factors have touched church involvement at every socioeconomic level, in rural, urban, and suburban churches alike.

In addition to cultural and economic factors causing church decline, other factors to consider in a church's decline include demographic change (population migration), institutional conflict or dysfunction, weak leadership, and a congregation's idolatry of its traditions and building. Let's consider the following factors.

13. Frykholm and Wuthnow, *The Christian Century,* para. 6.
14. Miltra Toossi, *Monthly Labor Review*, para. 3.
15. Kids Count Data Center.
16. Putnam, *Bowling Alone,* 19.

Demographic Change

Chinese Community Church has a long history of adapting to change. When I first visited with the church's matriarch, Gloria, I thought hers would be a sad story of a church that failed. Instead, I found a church that had practiced remarkable resilience and flexibility as it adapted to changes it could not always control.

Chinese Community Church has nearly one hundred years of history reaching out to Chinese immigrants and their families in its midwestern city. Ninety of those years have been witnessed by Gloria, whose father moved to the U.S. from China in 1915 to work as a tool and die maker in the automobile industry.

The mission with Chinese immigrants began when two active laywomen from a downtown Methodist church saw an opportunity for evangelism with the young immigrant workers and began teaching Bible classes in the church. The young men eventually sent for their families in China, and a small Chinese Christian mission took shape, supported by the church's long-time pastor. The mission provided English language classes and immigration assistance at first, and it eventually became a significant social gathering place for Chinese families. These were people without any Christian background before coming to the United States, so Christian education and baptism for all ages were emphasized. One of the church's assistant pastors was assigned to lead worship in English on Sunday afternoons. This mission continued for half a century, as the first generation raised and married off their American-born children.

In the 1960s, at the height of the postwar baby boom curve and the auto industry's expansion, the church became independently chartered within the United Church of Christ and purchased its own building in a working-class suburb of the city. There it enjoyed a brief period of growth. Its leader, a tent-making pastor who also worked as a lawyer, served the church for twenty-five years without pay, although the members on one occasion gathered an offering and bought him a new car.

By the end of the 1970s, it began to decline in size. Second-generation Chinese Americans were culturally different from their parents. The church was the only place in their daily lives where they were among other Chinese people and heard Cantonese spoken by the aunts and uncles. As they reached adulthood, these young people were educated and acculturated into an Anglo-American world. Many moved away and went to college.

The neighborhood began to experience ethnic change as more African Americans moved in.

In the early 80s, the congregation sold its building to an African American congregation and began renting space in another church's building. Two years later, it moved to a smaller space at yet another church, where the members worshipped on Sunday afternoons weekly. Today, about a dozen members meet in that church's lounge for worship once a month.

Gloria, who was born and baptized into Chinese Community Church, is now ninety years old. Her son is the president of the church and her daughter prints the bulletins. The church has a treasurer and a hired piano player, and it pays visiting preachers who are scheduled by Gloria herself. Offerings are no longer taken at worship, but the church has a small fund left from the sale of its building, which it uses to pay expenses to preachers and its host church. The members also manage two scholarship funds for Chinese-American college students and disperse annual gifts to UCC-related mission organizations. Their constitution now includes a plan for dissolution, a sort of "last will and testament," which details how their remaining funds will be dispersed.

Gloria is stoic about the changes her congregation has been through in its ninety-five-year history. She is deeply grateful for the Christian community she enjoyed through her lifetime, and, like many elderly Christians, she is perplexed about the younger generation's lack of interest in the social benefits of church affiliation. But the series of physical relocations were seen with a practical eye on necessity.

I was reminded, listening to her church's history, of the fact that this congregation's character was shaped by a people who had chosen and adapted to massive cultural and geographic change in their lives. Its founders were men and women who chose to develop new vocational, language, and social skills in a foreign land and were even able to open their hearts to a new religious belief and practice. This generation embodied the stories of Abraham and Sarah, Moses and Miriam.

"So many of our key people have passed away. We're just dying off. That's sad," Gloria says wistfully. But she also recognizes that her church was built for a particular time, place, and set of circumstances that no longer exist.

"When I'm gone, that's the end of the old church," she says. That comment can be heard two ways: as a self-centered expression of a matriarch who "owns" the ministry because of her own personal longevity and faithfulness to it, or as an honest appraisal of a ministry's limited lifespan.

Gloria's experience has been repeated in urban churches that sprang up in the nineteenth and twentieth centuries to serve migrating ethnic populations, from German Evangelicals to Mexican Pentecostals. Many of the churches I studied found it difficult, if not impossible, to repeat their early success attracting members when the first one or two generations had passed away. "They could never change that original footprint," one pastor said of her congregation after it closed.

While the character of Chinese Community Church made it adaptable to the changing circumstances of its Chinese immigrant members, it was a personality so firmly rooted in the Chinese experience of that first generation that it could not adapt culturally to a neighborhood quickly becoming inhabited by another ethnic group. Several churches that I interviewed, like Chinese Community Church, chose to adapt to their situation by selling their buildings and moving to new neighborhoods. But in most cases, while effective ministry was extended for a number of years, there was no significant revitalization, only an adaptation to decline.

Institutional Dysfunction

While every church today is facing demographic and cultural shifts, some churches respond to the challenge in negative ways that lead them into a further downward spiral. It is important for congregations to examine how their own behavior may be contributing to loss of vitality.

When I first met Diane, she told me she had been part of a church that closed. "That church really *needed* to close," she said. When I asked her why, she described a pervasive lack of trust among the membership. While some leaders tried to be open in their communication, others reverted to secretive dissent, refusing to voice their opinions openly. "It was impossible to have open conversation about what to do. You always felt like someone didn't trust you."

After years of decline, it became obvious to Diane that they needed to talk about it. But whenever the question of closure surfaced, people said things like "Where will I be buried?" or "I've supported this church financially. They owe it to me to stay open."

A church like Diane's may react to changing circumstances with a defensive attitude and a code of silence, blocking healthy responses to change and anxiety. Such behaviors might include silencing minority voices, avoiding decisions that involve risk, persistent conflict among members, or repeated developing of action plans that are never carried out. We will consider this kind of behavior more in chapter 3.

Leadership Issues

It is too often a temptation to blame the pastor for decline. Loss of membership and vitality is caused by a complex web of factors, and high expectations may be placed on a pastor who simply cannot deliver the miracles needed to turn a church around. But in some churches, poor leadership is a contributing factor in their decline:

- A revelation of clergy misconduct or a small group of belligerent lay leaders may drive members away, leaving the remainder without the critical mass needed to continue.

- Sometimes, a theological mismatch between the pastor and congregation creates unresolvable tension.

- A micromanaging pastor may exert so much control over a congregation that, when he or she departs, the congregation has lost the ability to govern itself.

- Lay or clergy leaders may panic or become numb in the face of an institutional crisis.

While most churches have survived a bad match with a pastor or even a case of clergy misconduct in their history, frail churches today may be toppled by a period of weak leadership at the crucial moment when strength and wisdom are needed.

The Idolatry of Structures

It is perhaps inevitable that, after decades or even centuries of maintaining church institutions with their stone foundations, payrolls, endowments, and seasonal rituals, they become self-propelled ships that are difficult to redirect for a new course in a new time. Powerful forces are at work in our churches to resist change. Church leaders must recognize that sometimes these forces lack integrity. When the focus of the church's energy revolves around property maintenance or local rituals that are no longer feasible, when care for the "family" comes at the expense of ministry to the community, we have turned our institutions into idols. Each church must do its own soul searching as to whether we have made gods of our institutional structures and traditions.

The last several decades of decline have led us to a time of confusion in the local church. What is our mission, exactly? Should we preserve the traditions that were so valuable to our parents' generation or redirect our mission to meet the challenges of our children's generation? If we turn outward toward the community, are we turning our backs on our members? Is it our fault that we are in this mess? Is it our parents' fault, or our children's?

UCC consultant and author Anthony Robinson has written, "As we anxiously monitor our losses and watch the bottom line, as we complain about the Religious Right or the mega-churches and self-righteously claim that we are the true-blue and truly enlightened, have we missed or misinterpreted what God is doing as Christendom and modernity decline and a new world emerges?"

Robinson asserts that "too many churches have been successful in turning their congregations into clubs." He notes that we engage in a "blame game" between pastors and parishioners, and that we continually look outward for a "silver bullet" that will solve our problems, instead of looking inward to examine how we might engage in adaptive change.[17]

The decline of churches over the last fifty years is the inevitable result of a changing cultural and demographic landscape. But it is also about the church's gradual loss of its own clear purpose. A once strong institutional anchor has become unmoored, and we are forced to reexamine our mission and our methods for carrying that mission out.

BETWEEN MOVEMENT AND SETTLEMENT

The history of God's people is fraught with tension between the call to migrate and the urge to settle down, and the Bible reflects this tension. Abraham and Sarah were promised a nation, but they never really arrived there. The patriarchs saw God as a promise and a presence, marked by piles of stones in the wilderness. The holy place was just a stone pillow and the dream of a ladder that permeated the "thin place" from which angels descended. Yahweh was a moving target, a swirling cloud, a fiery pillar, a holy box carried through the desert, wary of staying too long in one place, and eager to prove to humanity that, when they traveled into new territory, their God would still be with them.

17. Robinson, *Changing the Conversation*, 40–44.

At the same time, it is only natural that God's people long for a homeland. The slaves freed from Egypt were motivated by a promise of a new life in Canaan. The portable Covenant Box was eventually housed in a resplendent temple that conveyed immutability. The wandering nomads, guided by their trust in Yahweh, were transformed into a nation with borders, protected by soldiers and governed by human kings.

That nation and its temple were later toppled and sent into exile. Centuries later, a second temple was destroyed yet again. But today, thousands of pilgrims still flock to the ruins of the temple to tuck paper prayers into its decaying walls. They, like millions before them, bury a little piece of their hearts in its foundation.

The early church grew up in the shadow of the fallen temple. The Apostle Paul, sensing the cosmic shift in his own culture, wrote to the young churches, inviting them *not* to rebuild their beloved temple, but to engage in a different kind of building: to become "living stones," building the church with Christian character and acts of mercy instead of mere stone.

The history of God's covenant with us has carried us through periods of both settlement and wilderness wandering. And that story has not ended. We keep building stone foundations; and God keeps beckoning us back into the wilderness to hear the pure word of truth, to be fed by ravens and angels and to rediscover who and whose we are. The decline we are seeing now in the life of institutional churches is part of the greater story of how God keeps nudging us out of our comfort zones and on to that better country. It is our task to keep moving forward with trust, even when we're not sure where we are headed.

Toward the Better Country

REFLECTION

Then the Lord appeared to Abram, and said, "To your offspring I will give this land." So he built there an altar to the Lord, who had appeared to him. From there he moved on to the hill country on the east of Bethel, and pitched his tent, with Bethel on the west and Ai on the east; and there he built an altar to the Lord and invoked the name of the Lord. And Abram journeyed on by stages toward the Negeb.

Genesis 12:7–9 (NRSV)

Abraham and Sarah were called to a nomadic life in the wilderness living in tents, instead of a settled life behind the walls of a fortified city.

- Reflect on times in your life when you were "settled" and times when you were "nomadic" (for example, a move to another town or an immigrant experience). How have you maintained your relationship with God in these different seasons of your life?

- With a group, reflect on how your congregation has experienced both settlement and wilderness experiences in its history. What were some of the challenges and blessings of these different periods and where are you now?

- What signs have you seen that God is present with your congregation in your current state?

3

Expressions of Grief
in the Faith Community

*We know that the whole creation has been groaning in labor pains
until now; and not only the creation, but we ourselves, who have the
first fruits of the Spirit, groan inwardly while we wait for adoption, the
redemption of our bodies. For in hope we were saved. Now hope that
is seen is not hope. For who hopes for what is seen? But if we hope for
what we do not see, we wait for it with patience.*

ROMANS 8:22–25 (NRSV)

IT'S DIFFICULT TO FIND any mainline church that is not experiencing some
kind of loss these days. While a few denominations and new church developments are growing, and some churches are maintaining their membership, many have seen a significant decrease in resources: volunteer energy,
financial giving, and overall ability to carry out past programming. This
means that many churches, even those that are not facing imminent death,
are experiencing waves of grief related to various types of loss.

Rev. David Schoen, who works in the area of congregational vitality
and discipleship for the United Church of Christ, surprised me early in
our interview by stating that "the average lifespan of any church is about
eighty years." Yet, most of us think of churches as being permanent fix-
tures in the neighborhood. The shrinking or closure of a church violates

our sense of what we are supposed to be about. Churches are supposed to *grow*, we assume, or at least maintain a steady membership base as the young are baptized and the old pass away. We come from a tradition that values endurance and expansion. What Jesus started with twelve disciples mushroomed into a movement that spread across the globe. And he left us with that challenge: *Go and make disciples of all nations.*

When a congregation with a history of fruitful ministry experiences a downward spiral, the result is a profound disconnection and sense of failure. Although God has called you to share the gospel, you may no longer have enough money to pay the pastor or repair the building. Your fellowship is diminished as people stop coming or pass away. And the gospel you once cherished rings hollow in your ears when you sense that it is no longer "producing fruit" by attracting new members.

For congregations that have withstood decades of ups and downs, it's difficult to believe that, this time, you may not weather the storm. Simply coming to terms with the decline your church has already experienced is a difficult first step that will lead to various forms of corporate grief.

EXPRESSIONS OF GRIEF

Alongside the organizational challenges of church decline, which we will examine in upcoming chapters, struggling congregations are experiencing underlying personal grief and spiritual struggles that must be addressed if they are to move forward. Michael Weldon, who researched the reaction of Catholics to parish consolidations, has written,

> The main reason why religious congregations, parishes, or dioceses resist renewal is a failure to mourn or ritually detach themselves from "that which is lost" or "no longer apostolically relevant."[1]

Research on grief has identified various emotions experienced by people who have lost a loved one or received a diagnosis of terminal illness. These expressions include shock or denial, isolation, yearning for the lost loved one, anger, guilt, bargaining, depression, and recovery or acceptance.[2] The Hospice Foundation of America counsels,

1. Weldon, *A Struggle for Holy Ground*, 82.
2. Maciejewski et al., "An Empirical Examination of the Stage Theory of Grief," para. 7.

It is best not to think of grief as a series of stages. Rather, we might think of the grieving process as a roller coaster, full of ups and downs, highs and lows."[3]

Grief can also impact the functioning of congregational systems. In my own experience with a church in decline, I saw grief manifested in the congregation's ways of functioning, but I didn't always know how to read those signs. As you review the expressions of grief in this chapter, reflect on the signs you and your congregation may be seeing.

Denial

Stuart is a regional church leader who told me about a church that waffled in its acceptance of its own demise. When the church dwindled down to three elderly members, they called Stuart for help in closing the church once and for all. "We're tired," they told him.

Stuart led them through the administrative steps to closure. The Sunday of their closing service was well attended by former members who came back to celebrate the church's ministry. The sacred objects were ritually removed and passed on to other churches. It seemed to Stuart to be an honorable farewell.

But the next day, he returned to his office and took a phone call from one of the three former members. "It was so wonderful to see the church full of people again yesterday," she said. "Maybe we should stay open after all!"

While many of us are aware of church decline occurring in our culture, it's more difficult to recognize it in our *own* churches. We have a tendency to continue with familiar programming and traditions, overlooking the extent to which interest and participation has diminished.

In one of my churches, I presented the leaders with financial data that showed their annual budget had dropped by 20 percent in real dollars over the last five years. They nodded as if they were not surprised by this number. Yet, two weeks later, when I suggested they rethink their stewardship education methods, they insisted that the old pattern was still working.

Denial is a common response to loss. Denial indicates that the psyche is unable to integrate the reality of change or loss at the speed that change is occurring. In some people, a sort of "freezing" occurs that renders them unable to adjust their behavior to new circumstances. Peter Steinke has

3. Hospice Foundation of America, "Grief," para. 5.

written, "When facing anxious times, a high percentage of congregations freeze. Since action might trigger opposition, leaders delay and delay."[4]

In the midst of this delay, as tension mounts, members may engage in behavior that creates the appearance that "everything is still okay." Hoarding cash reserves or "hiding" designated funds in separate accounts are ways a congregation can maintain a state of denial about its financial situation. Stressed leaders may fail to do the analysis necessary to show that their reserves are depleting at a rapid rate.

June was the moderator at Immanuel Church during its decline. Although the membership had declined steadily for a couple of decades, the congregation continued to hire full-time pastors in the hope that the ministry could be revived. As funds dwindled, one lay leader kept repeating an old truism of the church: "We've been through tough times before. Someone will step up to see us through." But what had been true in the past was not true for the present. One Sunday, June revealed to the congregation that they only had enough money to pay their current pastor for two more months, after which the church's reserves would be depleted. When June reported this story to me several years later, I asked her why it took so long to see the severity of the church's financial state. Her eyes glazed over a little as she said, "I really don't know."

After years of decline, during which closure of the church was only hinted at in hushed tones, Pastor Lynn's governing board gathered data from members about the state of the church by forming small group meetings with parishioners. At the meetings, older member mainly reminisced about the past, but the younger members expressed concern about the education program. It had grown so small that the few families left were exploring other options for their children's Christian education. When this feedback came back to the chair of the education committee, he said, "There's nothing wrong with our Sunday School. We just need more kids."

While financial problems can alert a congregation to an impending crisis, human energy may be another resource in short supply. A few passionate, energetic leaders, including the pastor, may attempt to prop up a declining system by overfunctioning to keep up the appearance of a vital church. While this may work for a while, gradually the increased stress on a few members will topple what has become a house of cards.

Behaviors to watch for among those in denial also include: programs spearheaded and carried out by one person, heroic giving by one member

---

4. Steinke, *Congregational Leadership in Anxious Times*, 13.

to continue a program that has lost broad support, staff salary freezes, and an obsession with minor administrative details, just to name a few.

The delicate issue here is that churches for centuries have survived tough times with precisely the kind of resilience that may now show up as resistance to needed change. It may be difficult to discern how loyalty to a faith community through tough times becomes addiction to something that needs to die.

At Pastor Lynn's church, two members of the governing board began assuming the duties of other leaders who were slowly checking out in the midst of mounting anxiety. Each of these leaders volunteered to take on the duties of other lay leaders who had resigned. The remaining board members cooperated with this ruse, since they were no longer willing to fulfill their own obligations. But the resulting decision-making process quickly became a comedy of errors. At one governing board meeting, only two lay leaders showed up. Pastor Lynn moderated while one board member made motions, and the other seconded them. Then the two would vote. Besides the obvious fact that there was not a quorum present, the pastor recognized the acute illness that had taken over her congregational system and drove home from the meeting in tears.

It is also tempting for pastors to take on inappropriate roles in a declining church. Loretta, an executive presbyter (EP), recounted the story of one of the churches in her region during its last days. She attended the church one Sunday and found the pastor "did everything." He played the organ, took the collection, and preached. "It was one of the saddest things I ever experienced," she said. A busy church is not the same as a vital and viable church. Being busy at the tasks of keeping things going may distract us from examining what is truly happening in our midst.

Lay leaders and pastors are not the only ones to engage in denial about church decline. Denominational leaders are among those who have chosen to avert attention away from statistics about decline in favor of pushing for ambitious revitalization strategies. Any casual review of literature on local church ministry will show that, while all the statistics on decline are clear, most denominations still persist in teaching only strategies for growth and new church development. Few are openly addressing the need of some churches to close. Sadly, as denominational structures have begun to experience their own downsizing due to dramatic losses in wider church giving, regional leaders are being forced to do the soul-searching that will lead us out of denial and into a new realm of acceptance and adaptation.

Among waves of rapid change and compounding grief, denial is the little piece of wreckage we cling to in order to stay afloat. While denial may look like irrational behavior, it is a coping strategy necessary to the work of grief. The danger comes when denial is allowed to permeate the community and create a code of silence, robbing the congregation of the opportunity to deal honestly and creatively with its own circumstances.

In some unhealthy churches, denial reigns for years, as a few members step up their commitment and pursue ever more frantic activity to maintain existing programs. Indeed, it could be said that, if it weren't for denial, many churches would not have lasted as long as they have. But if decline is sustained, leaders and the systems they maintain will eventually become exhausted. It usually takes a crisis or a novel opportunity to wake up the congregation in denial. In congregations I studied, crises came in the form of unexpected building repairs, internal conflict, or the loss of a spiritual patriarch, major donor, or long-term pastor.

Anger, Blame, and Shame

Once a crisis occurs that forces a church to face its situation, new grief reactions may surface. These emotions surface in different people at different times and make for a challenging mix of emotions for a leader to navigate.

Church members who are beginning to realize their church is facing a "critical moment" of needed change may look for someone to blame for their predicament. In the 90s, the common refrain was to blame the evangelical mega-churches for offering "church lite" to suburbanites who had no real interest in commitment and spiritual depth. Some blame their denominations for having become too "liberal" theologically. Older members may blame the younger generation for their lack of participation. Recently, the decision by some denominations to authorize gay and lesbian Christians for ordained ministry has been seen as a cause of turmoil leading to further decline.[5]

Who is to blame when a church experiences irreversible decline? Accusations may come from many directions and often imply to a congregation that, if they had just worked harder, or made one better decision, they could have prevented their own demise.

5. Some statistical loss of churches reported by denominations in recent years can be attributed not to closure, but to churches transferring out of their denominations on theological grounds. See, for example, "PCUSA Membership Drop in 2012."

Wayne, the lay leader at St. Paul's Church, recalled one interim pastor who repeatedly chastised his congregation from the pulpit for not working hard enough. This message came after years of effort and creativity on the part of the church's core leaders, who had attempted to relocate and revitalize the church in a changing urban neighborhood. Needless to say, the pastor's criticism of the congregation was not well taken.

While blame works for some people, others will turn inward to feelings of shame and regret about their part in a church's losses. Older members may harbor deep shame that they have been unable to keep their adult children in the church. Others will apologize for their own limited energy. One member of a dying church confessed to me, "I keep giving more every year, but it's never enough."

In one congregation, a large building project was undertaken, but the hoped-for growth of the congregation did not occur. Years later, a lay leader who had spearheaded the project confessed to me his shame that he had promoted an expensive project that did not provide the desired results. "I pushed for it, and it was a mistake," he said, as if the church's decline was his personal responsibility.

Pastors will sometimes blame themselves, even in congregations that do not hold them accountable, and this self-blame may lead to burn-out and depression. Pastor Dan was called by his regional pastor to serve a two-point charge. When he arrived, it became clear that one of the two churches was breathing its last breaths. The congregation and its previous pastor had been avoiding the issue for years. With the blessing of his district superintendent and church leaders, he began the administrative process of closing the church. But one inactive member resurfaced and began harassing him, accusing him of "coming here to kill our church." Not a single member of the church came to the pastor's defense. Three years later in our interview, Pastor Dan was still tearful about the psychological trauma this caused him. "You're put into it in its last stages. It's like you're a physician with a cancer patient with stage four cancer. I'm glad I'm retiring. I can't go through that again."[6]

---

6. Ironically, shortly after this interview, the pastor retired and was diagnosed with stage four cancer.

Bargaining

"Bargaining" is said to be a time of experimenting with behaviors that may delay death. While it is healthy for congregations to look for solutions as their vitality and viability wane, some will cling only to quick fixes that maintain the status quo. Anthony Robinson calls these "silver bullets":

> The silver bullet is the agent that will kill the enemy or magically solve our problems: it may be the perfect pastor, a better building, or new church home, the right youth program or youth director, having more money, even changing denominations, or {fill-in-the-blank}. More often than not, the problem is not "out there," not external to us. It is internal to us. Usually a change in our hearts and our minds is required.[7]

Regional pastors told me that a common request of struggling churches is simply for "life support": assistance from the wider church to keep their churches open. Heroic giving is another way churches stave off an impending disaster. At St. Paul's Church, lay leader Wayne told me how the building was finally sold after a long period of decline, and the congregation made a temporary agreement to rent space at Resurrection Church, located nearby. Since Resurrection Church was also struggling, this experiment might have led to a new way of being the church together. But in the anxiety that accompanied that transition, a wealthy member of St. Paul's made a large donation on the condition that it be used to purchase a new building in his neighborhood. The congregation moved, but the relocation was more than the tiny group could sustain for more than a few years. Sadly, both St. Paul's and Resurrection eventually closed, in part because both were in denial about the level of decline they were experiencing.

Churches in a state of bargaining know at some level that their days are numbered, but they remain open through creative strategies such as hiring part-time pastors, charging rent to community groups, or other means. While these strategies are in some ways adaptive, they are usually focused on the institution's survival, not on its missional growth. Congregations see these strategies as "buying time," negotiating for a few more years to function with their familiar traditions and the close fellowship they have come to love.

There are pros and cons about a church functioning in a state of bargaining. In some cases, churches have thrived for their entire lifespan at a

7. Robinson, *Changing the Conversation*, 44.

very small size and can do so effectively. For the maintenance of a unique ethnic or theological heritage, it may be worthwhile to let a congregation "bargain with God" to continue its ministry. But if the congregation has lost significant vitality, faithfully relinquishing God's gifts is an act of good stewardship that should be considered. The church is not a museum to entomb the past; it is an incubator of God's future.

Anger, withdrawal, and conflict among members may occur in a church facing its own demise. Behaviors like blaming, shame, overfunctioning, and bargaining are signs that members and leaders are attempting to put off the inevitable sadness that comes with acknowledging the truth of their situation. Anxious parking lot conversations, tense personnel evaluations with staff, and critical messages from the pulpit may all result from what Weldon calls "unarticulated grief." As with any loss, the soul shuffles around looking for ways to avoid its own obvious need: the need to express sadness. Sadness is a dark stage that, while difficult to face, is necessary to the process of letting go and moving on. The longer we avoid it, the more damage may be done. Weldon writes that squelched emotion "encourages a host of culture-destroying behaviors, often including holding on to time-tested ways of living. But holding on strangles; letting go heals."[8] At some point, the expressions of healthy grief will include a time of letting go and giving way to deep sadness.

Depression

As a struggling church comes to terms with its situation, members will enter a time of sadness or depression. Sadness is not only uncomfortable; it seems to run counter to the gospel message of hope. We are people of the resurrection, and we may presume we should be thankful (read: cheerful) in all circumstances. But in fact, sadness is a necessary expression of grief in church life, just as it is in the lives of individuals.

There was one winter in my own ministry when I sensed that my days as the church's leader were numbered, and that the church itself would probably not live much longer, despite all our efforts and hopes. I recall leafing through boxes of old records, reams of minutes from meetings at which we had busily planned for outreach projects, fundraisers, and new mission projects. It all looked so ambitious at one time—and so futile now. At this point in the church's life, there was less to do. Committees had

8. Weldon, *A Struggle for Holy Ground*, 82.

disbanded. Many homebound members had passed away and there were fewer pastoral calls to be made. One night after work I went out to my car and found a murder of crows perched on the church roof, its steeple, and the cross. It was like something out of Hitchcock's film, *The Birds*. I took it as a sign of an impending death I could not control anymore. I had tried everything. I had to give up.

At the same time, the congregation was entering its own period of depression. This was communicated primarily in nonverbal ways, so it was difficult to measure. On Sundays, the mood of the sanctuary was gloomy and quiet. Lay leaders increasingly found reasons to be absent from meetings. At one governing board meeting, hungry for some acknowledgment of the congregation's mood, I asked the group, "People seem so quiet around here lately. What do you think that's about?" After a long silence, the bravest leader said, "Maybe it's the economy."

The leaders were not ready to articulate their grief, but by Easter, I knew that I had sunk into a depression. As I got out of the car that morning in the church parking lot, I immediately began to cry, thinking of the task ahead: announcing the miracle of resurrection to a dying congregation.

At some point, a few members may, with prompting, begin a conversation about the church's past as a way of acknowledging that the past is over. "Remember when we had thirty kids in Sunday School?" "Remember Anna Mae and George? I sure miss them." The ability to have this type of conversation is a sign that members are facing their own sadness in healthy ways. Churches I interviewed reported taking a renewed interest in their history at a certain point, recalling their successful ministries and wonderful saints, not in an effort to fashion a future for the church, but to recall the integrity of its past.

In chapters 8 through 10, we will explore healthy behaviors a church can engage in to assist members with grief work, including seeking a strong leader or consultant, engaging in intentional conversation about the future, connecting with the wider church, focusing on your continuing mission, and liturgical practices that foster spiritual strength.

THE SHIFT TOWARD ACCEPTANCE

Recently I was cleaning the costume room at our local community theatre with my friend Kris. Kris was diagnosed with cancer several years ago, and her condition was labeled as terminal. But Kris is still alive. Although she is no longer able to work at her job as a nurse, she receives radiation treatments on a regular basis while raising her teenage son and volunteering in the community.

I went to Kris when my sister was diagnosed with an aggressive cancer, and she helped me understand how a person with a limited lifespan can still live a joyful life each day, focused on the present moment. The day we were cleaning the costume room, Kris said, "You get to a point in your life when you just accept the fact that you're going to die."

"But my sister isn't there yet," I insisted. "She still believes the treatments will work; she still has hope that she won't die."

"But she *will* die," Kris said simply.

My heart skipped a beat. Did Kris know something about my sister's cancer that I didn't know? "How do you know that?" I asked in alarm.

"Because we all die someday," Kris replied. "The only difference for people with a terminal illness is that we know our lives are limited."

Pastor Mark and his congregation engaged in a lengthy discernment process, which you will read about in chapter 8. When they finally decided to close their rural church, he was ready to let go. He chose to enact his acceptance by doing a photographic inventory of the church's possessions before they were dispersed.[9] In an e-mail about the experience, Mark wrote:

> I shared the photos with some of the folks on Sunday morning, and they began remembering who made various banners, and who donated various objects. I encouraged them to write the names down. It was a way to recall the past and think about the things we have done together.
>
> I shared with them my feelings of sadness, and how I realized how much greater theirs could be, too. I saw a few heads nodding. There were less than 10 in worship yesterday—cold weather, blowing snow blocking country roads, people at home ill. That is a bit discouraging when I looked at all the white hair. I heard that someone who came several times in January commented to a frequent member that he wished he had come to church more often. Too little, too late. Well, we are grieving.

Some interviewees reported that, once a decision was made for merger, building sale, or closure, the ambiguity and unacknowledged grief was let loose, and the congregation found energy for the process of moving forward. The Blue River Presbyterian Church was located in a rural

---

9. An inventory of assets is required by some denominations, upon the closure of a church.

area, where it had shared a pastor with four other nearby congregations for several years. When that pastor was no longer available, the church had to decide how to proceed. They reflected on their history and recalled that their church had originally been built as an outreach to Scottish farmers. Later in history, the Scots moved to Iowa and German Lutherans bought up the farms in the area. The Germans started a Lutheran church and new residents went there. Once the members could retrace the trail of their history, there was a turning point. "We were here for the Scots," they said. The members drew on their thrifty Scottish character and concluded, "We can get the church we need without spending all this money here." They gave their building and remaining financial reserves to the adjoining rural cemetery as a perpetual endowment and began worshiping in one of their sister churches.

Specific actions that help move the church in the direction of acceptance can be carried out formally or informally. They might include a series of conversations concluding in a congregational vote, or a small gathering to recall memories and fondle the sacred objects that symbolize the church's history and character. The congregation might begin holding fellowship, choir events, or holiday services with a partner church it plans to merge with. They may celebrate the sale of a parsonage, or hold an anniversary celebration. These behaviors mark a church's acceptance of the fact that the church as it once was will no longer be.

In the best circumstances, these actions are taken in the firm hope that God is preparing a new frontier for the ministry. In some cases, however, a congregation will dig its heels in. One such case was that of St. James. They were so fiercely tied to their traditions and family affiliations that everything in the building had a memorial plate on it—even the photocopier's drum. But the congregation had dwindled to a dozen members managing a complicated web of designated funds and a building in need of repair. Pastors and presbytery advisers had come and gone, wounded by the level of resistance put up by the congregation. Deep denial had set in. When the denomination finally voted, against the will of the congregation, to close the church, the members literally walked away from the building, leaving its contents to be disposed of, and its frail elderly to be cared for by members of the regional body.

THE GROUP IN GRIEF

Grief may be difficult to recognize in a church because its various expressions hit different people at different times. While some members are overfunctioning, or simply struggling to keep buildings maintained and programs functioning, others will slip into a malaise or withdraw altogether. In my own leadership of an ailing church, this was the most confusing aspect of our decline. While some members were asking openly if the church was going to close, others were busily starting up new mission projects. In the midst of their various stages of grief, I stood in my own emotional maelstrom. One day I would feel driven to make some new program work. The next day, I would sit in the empty sanctuary with the heavy weight of futility on my heart. Inside me roiled all the mixed emotions of my congregation. With individual members in varying stages of grief, how does the congregation as a whole move forward?

CIRCLE THE WAGONS OR FLEE THE SYSTEM?

Church consultant and family systems expert Peter Steinke has written, "If intense and prolonged, anxiety has a strangling effect, depleting people's energy, disturbing their thinking, and dividing their loyalties."[10] If the natural human response to danger is "fight or flight," a threatened group of people will face similar choices. A congregation may experience division and implode from the inside, or it may do the opposite: turn inward for strength in a time of anxiety. In the latter case, some congregations choose to "bolt themselves to the floor" and maintain their traditions in defiance of encroaching threats.

Pastor Arlene led the St. James church mentioned above for a short time. She experienced this dying church as being extremely "rigid" in its behavior. One key lay leader dictated the proper behavior of the group, and everyone followed along. Leaders cooperated in hiding designated funds and in inaction when the church roof needed extensive repair. No pastor could penetrate this rigid, sick system with needed remedies.

When I arrived at my church, I asked them how they had coped with the stress of their recent decline and the firing of a previous pastor. "We circled the wagons," someone said. Tight-knit churches like these may rely

10. Steinke, *Congregational Leadership in Anxious Times*, 3.

on one another over and against outside forces such as a new pastor or a wider church body.

Other churches will experience division and alienation. A crisis can bring out the worst in us, and some members will withdraw, bitter about being used and spit out by their troubled church families.

EFFECTS OF CHRONIC ANXIETY

All congregations deal with anxiety at various times in the life cycle. But a church in decline may slip into what Steinke calls "chronic anxiety," so that anxious functioning becomes encoded in the behavior of the group.

Here are a few examples of behaviors your congregation may be displaying in its life together that indicate it is functioning with chronic anxiety:

- A "vampire church" may take shape, in which members, and even visitors, are viewed as "tools" in the continued maintenance of the church instead of souls to be cared for. Those who work hard for the church are rewarded and clung to as saviors. When a member leaves the system, those remaining silently calculate the cost of their departure in money and human energy. In a vampire church, the congregation functions to suck the life blood out of its members for its own survival.

- Creative leaders begin to exit the system, sometimes in a burned-out condition. New leaders have fewer leadership skills and, in some cases, greater anxiety about keeping the system running as it is.

- Pastoral leadership is compromised: the congregation may not be able to keep a skilled pastor for an extended period of time, either for financial reasons or because dysfunction is setting in.

- The sense of mission is lost: a congregation may repeat ritual activities without generating any spiritual energy. Outside of close personal relationships, no one can say why the congregation exists.

- Basic programming and maintenance of the building languish because of a listless leadership.

ANXIETY IN CLERGY

The stress level of clergy in all types of churches has risen dramatically in recent years. But the challenge of loving a congregation through anxiety and decline brings unique demands, even when there is no active resistance to closure. Neither pastor nor congregation can anticipate with certainty a long-term future for the church. While clergy do not always share the congregation's emotional attachment to the system, being the leader of a dying church will tax the pastor's self-esteem and shake his or her theological footing. In my interviews with pastors, I was especially struck by the depth of emotion that lingered even years after their experience of a closure. Several of them have since left local church ministry for chaplaincy, retired early, or experienced chronic health problems.

THE SINKING SHIP

My husband had a brother named Roy who was once a skipper on a crab fishing boat off the coast of Alaska. One day, his ship iced over in a storm and the crew lost control of the vessel. As the storm raged, Roy did everything in his power to keep the ship upright while making sure his crew got into their survival suits. However, he never got his own suit on, and he perished in the sea.

In the last year of my ministry in a struggling church, I often thought of Roy. I felt like a skipper, trying desperately to keep my little boat afloat. My husband gently suggested that the effort was getting the best of me, and that I might consider seeking a new call. But I resisted this, comparing myself to his brother Roy. "I'm the skipper," I said. "If I leave, it will be like I abandoned ship." My husband gave me a hard look. "Roy is dead," he said.

Churches that face prolonged anxiety strain the faith of their members and pastors, often to the point of burnout and abandonment. The institution that was built to foster spiritual growth and strength becomes a system that drains the spiritual energy from its members. The greatest tragedy in my mind is not so much the loss of churches, but the loss of faith and spiritual energy that occurs when God's gathered people switch their focus from life-giving ministry to artificial life support.

WHERE IS GOD?

Lucille raised four daughters and led youth programs in her small church before it closed. By the time I interviewed her three years later, she had become active in another church. "They're nice to me," she said sullenly. But when I asked her whether she saw God's hand anywhere in the closure process, she said no. "It kind of felt like God left us," she said. "I can't make sense of it. We tried so hard, but everybody gave up."

I pressed Lucille to think of stories from the Bible that might speak to her experience of a church dying, alongside her new life in the church she was now attending. She drew a blank. Finally, I reminded her of the story of Christ's death and resurrection. I was struck that, after a lifetime of hearing this story every Easter, she was still unable to apply it to her experience of losing a church.

How can the faith and vitality of Christians be restored and maintained, even as we lose the institutions that once housed and symbolized that faith? Ultimately, we must turn back to scripture to find our hope. We might imagine Christian history as a steady movement upward, from the first spark of creation to the final reconciliation in that "holy city seen of John." But on closer inspection, we see that the history of the church is a constant cycle of deaths and rebirths, as it moves forward in God's time.

God chose an infertile couple, Abraham and Sarah, to parent a new nation. Slavery in Egypt gave way to milk and honey in Canaan. The temple built by Solomon was destroyed by the Babylonians. The Savior sent by God was hung on a cross. The stone that the builders rejected has become the chief cornerstone (Psalm 118:22).

Faithful Christians do not insist on a pattern of continued upward "success" any more than Jesus did. Paul reminds us in Romans 8 that, in the midst of loss, we can also perceive the birth pangs of a new kingdom. Once we are able to face the change that is already happening around us, we may open our hearts to the possibility that God is yet at work in our struggling churches.

REFLECTION

For godly grief produces a repentance that leads to salvation and brings no regret, but worldly grief produces death.

2 CORINTHIANS 7:10 (NRSV)

- How do you feel when you hear that the average lifespan of a congregation is about eighty years? What do you anticipate will be the lifespan of your congregation?

- Tell stories about expressions of grief you have observed in your own life and that of your congregation's history. How have these various expressions affected your ability to make healthy decisions and move toward acceptance of change?

- Gather members in worship, a Bible study, or other setting to recall biblical stories of failures, losses, and grief and the ways God's people negotiated these experiences in history.

4

Discerning the Failure to Thrive: Lay Leaders

To whom shall I speak and give warning,
That they may hear?
See, their ears are closed,
They cannot listen.

JEREMIAH 6:10 (NRSV)

WHEN MY MOTHER WAS sixty years old, she came to the end of a five-year struggle with cancer. In her last days, she was given morphine to keep her comfortable, but she was unable to communicate with us. We sang to her, held her hand, and prayed for her. Sometimes when we were alone, I would sit by her bedside and watch her breathing, which was one of the few signs of life she had left. If she stopped breathing for a moment, I would breathe for her, as if it would help keep her alive. Then I would lean forward, waiting for the next comforting sign she was still with us.

Hospice workers speak of a condition known as "failure to thrive" in the elderly. In this condition, the mind and body slowly decline in functioning, leading to a state of malnutrition, increased physical disability, cognitive loss, and lowered immunity to infection.[1] In a physiological system like the human body, health care workers can identify specific signs that

1. Robertson and Montagnini, "Geriatric Failure to Thrive," 1.

the body is losing its ability to cope with disease or aging, and that a patient is proceeding toward death. At the same time, members of the family will often cling to those subtle but precious signs of life: the few bites of food taken, the mumbled words, the slow breaths.

With congregations, the signs that the institution is experiencing failure to thrive are more difficult to read. Like the children of aging parents, we focus instead on signs of life until the last breath is taken. It is natural to cling to the life of anything you love.

But loving children, even in grief, make plans for a dying parent's demise. Reading and responding to the signs of a coming death is part of our responsibility to each other, a way of honoring those we love.

In the church, accepting responsibility for the failure of a church to thrive is the work of three entities: the church's members, its pastor, and its wider church body. In this and the next two chapters, we will explore ways that lay leaders, pastors, and regional bodies can help a local church in decline fulfill its mission and discern God's plan for significant change or completion of a ministry. Reading about your own level of leadership will help you understand your own role. Reading about the other levels of leadership will give you ideas about what you can ask for or expect from your partners in the wider church. All three types of leaders can ideally work together to diagnose signs of decline and respond in healthy ways.

ME? A LEADER?

The average layperson may not think he or she is equipped to lead a church toward major change, but, in fact, you are the closest to your congregation's heartbeat, and you will be instrumental in any change that occurs. You have also played a role in your church's past. The health of any church, regardless of its life stage, depends more than anything on the spiritual health, insight, and vision of its members.

USING YOUR AUTHORITY

In my experience, there are two kinds of lay leaders: the ones who think they *are* in charge, and the ones who think they are *not* in charge. Claiming authority for lay leaders can be a tricky business. What is the source of your authority? And how should you use that authority without overfunctioning?

Churches have many kinds of leaders. There are *formal leaders*, like the governing board and the pastor. These are the recognized decision makers, but they are not always the ones pulling the strings. You might assume that real power lies in the hands of the formal leadership, but in many churches, formal leaders are heavily influenced by some of the other kinds of leaders mentioned below.

There are *spiritual leaders*. These are people whom the congregation has quietly acknowledged as faithful Christians, mentors, or guides. At First Presbyterian Church, Lorraine was the spiritual leader to whom everyone turned for wisdom and guidance. Her formal role was as the church's bookkeeper. But when it came time to make big decisions, even the church's "movers and shakers" deferred to Lorraine's wise judgment. Every church has some members who are spiritually grounded and wise, if others take the time to notice and listen.

Church *patriarchs* and *matriarchs* are another type of leader. These are people who have been part of the church since before anyone else can remember. Gloria, from chapter 2, was such a leader. These people carry the church's memories within them, and they may act as a sort of "anchor" for recalling the church's original purpose and significant turning points. Anchors can be a great gift in times when a church needs stability. They can also be an impediment when the church needs to sail in a new direction, unless they are willing to be unmoored.

Most churches have members who are *experts* in a given area of the ministry. Pastor Karl guided a church through closure and then started a new church development with a few members of the closed church. One particular member, Jack, felt ill-equipped for the financial leadership role he was thrust into when his tiny church was down to only a few members. But later, as the new church began to grow, Jack was asked to lead in the area of building maintenance, a role that fit with his experience as a plumber. Leaders can be tapped for their expertise as lawyers, real estate agents, social workers, financial managers, or nurses.

Finally, a leader who may be overlooked is the *outsider*. This person may be an inactive member, a very new member, or even a visitor. This kind of person can lead by asking novel questions: "Why do you do it that way?" "Why is this artwork here?" "What do your members believe in?" "Do you have a hands-on mission project I can get involved in?" or "How come you don't have coffee hours?" The outsider leads by asking questions an insider would never think to ask. And when asked, the insiders have to reflect on who they are and why they behave as they do. Sometimes, an interim pastor or consultant may serve as the outsider.

What is *your* unique leadership position? Is it a formal or informal role? How can you faithfully use that position to start a conversation about what you sense is happening in your congregation?

What other types of leaders exist in your fellowship? A discernment time is a good time to access the wisdom of voices that may not have been heard in the past. Because discernment can be accompanied by anxiety, asking everyone to tap into their own sources of spiritual, historical, and technical wisdom is a way to gain a sense of empowerment for the next steps you need to take. Every member of the church family needs to hear that their gifts were given not just for their own ego satisfaction or personal benefit, but for the glory of God. A time of transition is not the time to hold back!

"IS SOMETHING WRONG, OR IS IT JUST ME?"

Let's say you have a sinking feeling that something is wrong at church. Nothing dramatic has changed, but little by little, the energy has been seeping out of your congregation's fellowship and worship. Maybe people are bickering, or maybe they're just anxious. Maybe it's just your imagination. Maybe it's not.

I remember attending a fundraising event where a group of members was to gather at someone's home and make soup. When I arrived, only a couple of people had shown up. I pulled Nancy, a member I trusted, aside and said, "What's going on? How come all those people who promised to come didn't show?" She looked down and shook her head sadly. But her wordless reply told me all I needed to know: it wasn't just me. The congregation was stuck in a deep malaise. If I had not questioned her, both Nancy and I would have gone away wondering if it was "just us."

That question, *"Is something wrong at church?"* can make a person feel isolated—especially if no one else is talking openly about the problem. I have felt this way as a pastor and didn't know how to start a healthy conversation about what I was sensing. Even as the leader, I didn't want to be the one to "stir the pot." If this has been difficult for me as a pastor, I imagine it is even more difficult for lay leaders to be the first to ask, "What's wrong?"

WHEN IS THE RIGHT TIME TO START
THE CONVERSATION?

Maybe thoughts about your church's future have been gnawing at you for awhile, but you haven't found an opportunity to start the conversation. There is no right or wrong time to tell the truth, but some occasions can be used as opportunities.

The most obvious time for honest appraisal of your church's ministry is at the time of a pastoral transition. Churches of every size and shape can benefit from using an interim period and a specially trained pastor to reflect on their history and character, strengthen their ties to the wider church, inspire new lay leaders for service, and readjust their mission in a changing cultural context.

A church that is losing vitality and viability may be faced with important decisions at this point, whether they want to make them or not. For example, churches that have previously employed a full-time pastor will need to reexamine their sources of income and how the staffing configuration may need to change. If a part-time minister is hired, they will need to adjust their expectations of the staff and strengthen lay leaders' ownership of the ministry.

In some cases, staff must be asked to resign or a pastor's contract may need to be renegotiated. Pastor George served the tiny Hermans Presbyterian Church and another yoked parish faithfully for many years. He had struggled to keep the yoke together in part because he needed the health insurance this arrangement made possible. But the church was drawing down their reserves by $11,000 per year in order to keep up the building and pay a part-time salary. The session called their Executive Presbyter (EP), Gary, in a panic when they realized they only had $10,000 left in reserves. He went to visit the governing board and laid out several options: they could seek a trained lay pastor, merge with another church, or close their doors. A sigh of relief filled the room. "We've been thinking about closing," the clerk said. "But I was afraid to bring it up when Pastor George was here."

Any time when a significant change or decision is confronted, discernment questions can be given attention. Pastor Mark served a three-point parish for about a decade when one of his churches started showing signs of serious decline. During the planning of that church's centennial celebration, a member gave a donation to install a new stained glass window in the church. But church leaders were aware that the building was in decay and were doubtful about installing a new window into such an old structure. Someone asked, "What if we put the new window in, and then we close in five years?" The unspoken fear was revealed. From there, creativity broke open. It was decided that the new window would be housed in a moveable glass box and placed in the sanctuary. If the church moved or closed, the window box would be preserved and used in another setting. Pastor Mark likened it to the Covenant Box carried through the wilderness by the Israelites in Exodus 25.

Milestones in a church's life, from the death of a beloved matriarch to the repair of the roof, can be used as an opportunity to talk about what has meaning in the memories of members, and what purpose and mission they continue to stand for. These conversations reinforce the fact that your ministry has experienced success in sharing the gospel with its community. They should also lead to new questions like, "So, what are we doing now to fulfill our historic mission?" or "How would we carry out our mission if we didn't have a building or pastor?"

WHY DO I HAVE TO SAY IT?

While we are all wary of leaders who are pushy and controlling, it is equally damaging to a church's functioning when leaders are passive and refuse to speak about their own perceptions. A culture of silence can be just as oppressive as a dominating patriarch. Every leader must claim his/her own unique voice if the Holy Spirit is to have a chance at bringing life from a deathly situation.

Does raising questions about your church's vitality and viability mean you are the "grim reaper" or the prophet of doom? Not necessarily. Some church members try to silence conversation about decline because they think closure will be a "foregone conclusion" once they do. But talking about signs of decline does not always mean a church is destined to close. It means that the church is *already* experiencing change. Being the one to name that does not make you the "bad guy." You are fulfilling your role alongside biblical prophets like Isaiah and Jeremiah. For courage, read their writings and recall that, in the good times, they drew attention to the flaws in their community, but in the hard times, they revealed the underlying grace and power of God. It is your call to do the same.

The signs you read of change and decline may or may not be signaling the need to proceed with downsizing or closure. Facing the symptoms of decline helps a church learn about itself and its community, and take steps toward fulfilling God's purpose in new ways. Whether you downsize, revitalize, merge, or close your doors, your goal should always be faithfulness to God's purpose. In chapter 7, you will read about churches that have used their own decline as an opportunity for creative new ministry. The earlier you begin the conversation, the more options you will have to continue doing ministry together in some form.

WHO SHOULD I TALK TO?

Serious conversations about your church's viability and vitality can be difficult. The conversation may not lead to the kind of new life that everyone is wishing for. If you want to start this kind of conversation with a heart open to the Spirit's leaning, you will need partners. Who can you talk to?

Consider the voices of wisdom in your church. Don't be afraid to approach the pastor. As awkward as it may be to test out ideas that may lead to an ending to his or her livelihood, your pastor probably wants to know your perception of how things are going in the church, even if s/he doesn't share your view. If you are in a leadership position, you may want to float ideas with your leadership group: how are others feeling? Has anyone noticed the signs of malaise you are seeing? If you are feeling grief about the church's various losses, say it out loud. Maybe someone else is feeling that, too. If the leadership and pastor are both resistant to wider conversation, seek out a spiritual leader in the congregation whose opinions you value.

If you find there is no one in your congregation who wants to seriously engage in discernment about the church's future, you may want to start a conversation with a regional pastor who can share with your governing board his or her perception of their overall health. Keep in mind that your congregation and pastor know the church best. But your regional pastor is versed in what other churches are doing, national trends, and resources like this book. The best approach is to team wise leaders from all levels of the church if possible.

Not everyone will share your perceptions, and some may resist talking further about it. But you have opened a door to conversation and "broken the ice." If and when others are ready, the conversation will expand, and creative ideas for adaptive change may surface.

EARLY ADAPTORS

In the early 90s, Peter started seeing signs that his church was not growing. His passion was for youth ministry, so he proposed that some funds from a large endowment be used to hire a youth pastor to do outreach ministry for one year and see where it led. He had the support of another lay leader and they went to the pastor with their idea. The pastor, who had served the church for many years, didn't warm to the idea, and neither did the governing board. Shortly after this, the pastor moved to another church, and the decline Peter had anticipated began to increase.

Several pastors came and went, but none of them led the church into any serious discussion of their decline until the situation became dire. Peter, now the council chair, urged his pastor to send them a leader who had experience with church closures, and thankfully a suitable transitional pastor was sent. Peter was able to team with the transitional pastor to begin serious conversation about closure. The pastor listened to members of the congregation and helped them address the difficult question of whether they should close or perhaps merge with a church of the same denomination across town. Over a four-year period, the congregation prayed and discerned, along with their sister church, a course of action. Each year, a new question for reflection would be brought to the congregation at their annual meeting. Finally, the pastor enlisted the help of Maureen, a trusted lay woman who was a spiritual leader of the church. She stood up at a meeting and expressed her opinion that selling the building and joining their sister church across the river was the best course of action. Eventually, a healthy blending of the two congregations was accomplished.

Although Peter was an "early adapter" who saw the need for change before others did, his pastor taught him that the congregation would need to move at a slower pace in order to complete their former ministry with the right spirit and intention. Peter, his pastor, and Maureen were leaders who led by following.

Diane also recognized some early signs that her church was in decline. But she was given little authority and was not included in leadership decisions, even when she held an office. She attended training workshops on church growth with other members but noticed that the ideas they brought back were usually dismissed. She also noticed that the climate of worship became very dark and there were hushed meetings in the parking lot after worship. Whenever anything new was tried, she heard complaints. A new pastor was hired who tried to initiate a few changes and encourage more open communication, but she was met with resistance from some of the older membership.

Finally, Diane made what she calls the "hardest decision I have ever made in my life." She stood up one Sunday and announced she was leaving the church in two months. She listed her reasons for leaving openly. She offered to train anyone who would replace her as the chair of the worship committee she served on. She invited other members to talk to her about her decision, but no one did. After her departure, the organist and pastor also resigned. The church closed less than a year later.

While both these stories end differently, each displays for me a healthy lay leader taking initiative to address the different types of decline they were experiencing in their churches. They noticed the losses occurring around them, and they understood the reasons for decline. They responded by seeking out others who felt as they did and bringing new ideas to the table. They stayed true to their convictions and connected to their churches as long as they could, even when they met with resistance.

Both these faithful lay leaders went on to new ministry in new churches. Instead of letting a declining system take them down, they stepped out and acted to build Christ's body in healthy church families. You can do that too.

GATHER OBJECTIVE DATA

How should you begin to respond to the signs of decline you are sensing? First of all, as Stuart, a denominational leader, put it to me, "Get the facts. Information is something churches are so afraid of. The church only looks at information as a total last resort. Most decisions are made almost entirely emotionally."

Get the facts about your situation. But don't jump on one alarming fact and assume it spells catastrophe. What are the specific signs of decline you are witnessing? If worship attendance seems to be down, take a count, or go back and review old attendance records for comparison. Then assess reasons why this may be occurring. For example, are members traveling farther to attend? Are a stable number of members attending less often, making the worship space seem emptier?[2] Has the worship service taken on a somber tone?

2. See Bullard, "Is Attendance in Your Congregation Declining?"

If the financial crises seem to come more often, compare giving, spending, and membership records over the last few years to see if you can identify trends. Are fewer people giving, or are more people giving less money? Is the church bearing new financial burdens the congregation may not be aware of, like higher heat bills or salary increases that exceed giving increases?

Are you able to find lay leaders to fill various positions? Do lay leaders exert authority and creativity or rely on the pastor to tell them what to do? Does the pastor work as a partner with lay leaders?

Your church's neighborhood is also unique. What types of losses have occurred in your community? Is the neighborhood aging or changing ethnically? Has there been a plant closure or a school consolidation? Have any other churches in your area closed?

How does the congregation express its mission in the world? Who, outside of your own congregation, values your presence and purpose? What is your reputation in your community? Who would miss you if you closed your doors?

Be cautious about assumptions. The size of your worshiping group, for example, may not indicate that your church is "in trouble." Some very small churches are also very vital. The fact that you cannot afford to maintain your building does not necessarily mean you have a "stewardship problem." It may simply mean your building is too expensive for your congregation at its current size. And don't assume that, just because everyone in your current membership is happy with things as they are, your church is vital and viable.

When assessing your church's vitality and viability, focus on recent past performance, not what you wistfully remember from your "glory days," or ambitious plans for the future. Consider ministries you are engaged in now that touch the lives of people outside your membership. Consider whether any of your mission projects involve action other than the writing of checks. Has the congregation proved in the past that it can adapt to change? Has it ever engaged in risk-taking ventures that were allowed to fail?

Most importantly, like any mature Christian, a faith community should strive to think less about its own welfare and more about caring for its neighbors. Reflect with others on the needs of your community. Where are the pockets of poverty, loneliness, or injustice? Who in your community is being ignored or shunned? Ideas for studying your neighborhood might include "prayer walks" around the community looking for God's activity, or meeting with community leaders like school counselors, police, and health care workers.

Go back and look at your church's historic mission, and your effectiveness at articulating and pursuing it. As you consider the church's changing mission field, ask yourself what God is calling you to do and be at this time.

What is needed at this point are more good questions and less shallow answers. While it is difficult to maintain objectivity about something you are as fiercely attached to as your church, objective data gathering is a vital reality check for discerning your future. When emotions run high, anxiety can be tempered with hard information, and more sound decision making can occur.

USE EVERYONE'S GIFTS

The process of gathering data about your congregation's health is your chance to make use of the gifts of other lay leaders. Each of them may be privy to objective signs of decline that other members, the pastor, or a regional leader would miss. A Sunday School teacher may be the only one who can tell the truth about how many children are in Sunday School each week. The church secretary may file the worship attendance records, but maybe nobody pulls them out to review. Perhaps you are the only one who still lives in the neighborhood and you may have the best sense of community needs. A real estate agent in your membership may have a feel for the value of your property, which should be considered a significant asset. If you are the treasurer, you may keep records of many, tiny memorial gifts that no one else cares to examine at the church's annual meeting. The nominating committee chair is always searching for potential leaders and probably has a directory with names crossed off: members who have moved away, died, or become inactive. Who else is paying attention to this list? One or two leaders are hopefully in contact with denominational leaders and may understand the wider church's parallel struggles over finances, staffing, and the changing mission field. Are you one of the few members who attends worship every Sunday? Or one who only comes a couple of times a year? Either type of worshipper may have insight into how the mood of worship has been changing over time, and what that might signal about the spiritual health of the congregation.

And what about the inner circle, the governing board, which feels the pulse of the congregation on a weekly basis? Is this group talking openly about its observations with each other, and with the congregation?

Anyone with good financial sense can look at the church's sources of income and expenses to discern how money is flowing, as long as all sources of income and expenses are transparent. Some churches rely heavily on a few elderly givers. Others rely on rental income from nonprofit organizations. Many are dipping into reserves given by past generations. Will your main sources of income continue to flow for years to come, or will they be drying up soon? Where else can you turn for financial resources? What is your building and property worth? How much would your deferred maintenance cost if you actually had the repairs done? If you continue to draw funds out of your reserves at the rate you are now, how many months or years will the funds last?

A financial assessment like this was the moment of truth for First Presbyterian Church. They had no significant savings or endowments but had always made ends meet, until the last year of their life together. Their only nest egg at that point was a bequest, with no strings attached, which had been given by Lorraine, the beloved spiritual leader of the church, after her death. The congregation looked grimly at their options in the eleventh hour: they could close their doors now, or stay open for another year or two, using up Lorraine's gift. Knowing about the faith of Lorraine, they could not rationalize using her gift for their own survival and chose instead to close their doors and allow the gift to be permanently invested in a denominational mission fund.

TAKE STOCK OF YOUR ASSETS

As you engage in discernment, be sure to take note of your spiritual and material *assets*, not just your losses. What gifts are still contained in your congregation? How is your church proclaiming a unique theological message that your community values? Is there a long-time mission or education ministry that would be sorely missed if you were gone? What unique mission might your building fulfill in the neighborhood if it was used differently?

When Peter's church was discerning whether to join with its sister church across town, he went to visit the other church and noticed that "they couldn't sing over there to save their lives!" His church, on the other hand, had many musical gifts. As the two churches made a plan for blending their ministries into one, they began producing a joint choir concert every Christmas. Peter anticipated that his church, while giving up its building, would bring its musical gifts to the new church and teach them how to sing. And that they have done.

CONSIDER YOUR COMMUNITY MISSION

Almost every congregation has a mission legacy in its neighborhood. What is yours? Are you a gathering place for local nonprofit groups? Does your church house a food pantry or Boy Scout troop? What will happen if that legacy is taken from the neighborhood? Can it be carried on in some new way?

Gloria's church included in its constitution a "last will and testament" of sorts that bequeathed their Chinese student scholarship fund to the regional church body, where it would be administered into the future for any Chinese UCC student who applied. This arrangement satisfied the congregation's historic commitment to support the education of Chinese students long after the members were all gone.[3]

Some legacies cannot be continued without the presence of a faith community. Your church's unique theological voice or style of worship may not be replicated by any other church in your town. An inner-city church or a rural Native American congregation that reaches a population not served by other churches may leave a gaping hole if its mission outpost is uprooted. In some cases, the wider church should be approached about helping you sustain a significant mission outreach with financial support if it is vital, yet not financially sustainable.

MAKE USE OF DISCERNMENT TOOLS
AND CONSULTANTS

While your regional pastor will want to know about discernment conversations you are engaged in, s/he may not have the time to give full attention to your process. (Wider church bodies are dealing with their own downsizing issues!) Using this book and the resource list included, seek out other tools to guide your conversation.

3. See chapter 9 for information about Legacy Trusts, a way of passing on church assets with specifications for their use in future mission projects.

A study resource will help your members hear the messages emphasized in the introduction: *you are not alone, it's not all your fault, and you are not a failure.* If you think you may need leadership for a discernment process, you can enlist the assistance of a church consultant or facilitator to guide your conversation. Contact your regional body or those of similar denominations to make contact with their staff or a trained facilitator who can guide you through a discernment process.

A quality resource or consultant will not give you "an answer" that will save your church. But these resources will help you listen to one another and God as you consider where you are and where you need to be going.

Studying the hard data may cause you to face some bad news you would rather ignore. But it may also help your congregation find unexpected hope in your circumstances. Ignoring the data only leads to more anxiety.[4]

PUT THE DATA ASIDE AND LISTEN TO THE HOLY SPIRIT

There comes a time to put away membership records and financial charts and listen to another voice: that of the Holy Spirit. Instead of simply brainstorming about what *you* want to do, pray about what God wants. Better decisions are made when congregations engage in spiritual discernment, listening to God's voice in the process. Spiritual discernment might come through prayer circles asking "What is God leading us to do and be in this time?" Your group might do *lectio divina* study, where you read scripture and listen for what it may be saying in your congregation's current situation. You could try a Quaker-style meeting with some ground rules, where conversation is laced with silence and listening. God can speak through individuals in reflection and through groups in contemplative dialog.

Ask your pastor or a gifted member to lead such a group in prayerful discernment. Believe it or not, it *is* possible to hear and feel the urging of the Spirit. That is what prayer is for! The Spirit will not necessarily give you a clear plan, but it will help you to know God's yearning for you so that you can take the best next step in that direction.

---

4. Chapter 5 includes a list of questions you might use to begin evaluating your church's institutional and spiritual health. Some denominations also offer their own assessment tools and consultants, or see the Additional Resources section at the end of this book for more ideas.

Neither objective data nor spiritual listening can stand alone. Balance the spiritual work with data reality checks. On this topic, Stuart, a regional pastor, said pragmatically: "You can always trust the Holy Spirit, but it sometimes really helps to know what the actual situation is."

We have all seen how irrational anxiety can sweep through a group experiencing change. In high anxiety, poor decisions are made. With attention to God's voice, and the objective data, the body of Christ can lower its heart rate and discern with more wisdom.

EXPECT RESISTANCE

Perhaps the most difficult part of starting conversations about significant change is the sense that you have become a traitor, the church's enemy, by suggesting that significant change or even closure should be considered. You may incite the wrath of people you love. The message that "something needs to change" may be heard offensively by some as "What we have been doing isn't any good," even when you don't mean it that way.

When Peter first spoke of his sense that his church might need to close, some of the older members responded with expressions of loyalty to their building. "But we love our pretty church," they told him. Peter had to stay true to his message while also learning compassion for the older members who, he admits, had a much different experience of the church's history than he did. In retrospect, he said,

> It's harder for the elderly. They remember a better time. They re-
> member the 50s and 60s, when all the kids were in Sunday School
> and we had youth groups and women's groups. Our memories, the
> 50-year-olds, are different, it's not such a big part of our lives as it
> was for them."

At Pastor Bob's church, there was also some resistance to closure from an older contingent of the membership. Younger members, who were ready to move on, approached the older group as a team and said, "We want to stay and help you close if that is what is decided. But if you decide to stay open, you need to know that we will be leaving. We need churches with programming for our children. We need other people our age. You will have to go on without us." That may be a harsh message to an outsider's ears, but it was the truth told in love. When the older members tried to imagine moving ahead without the younger, they decided to close their church and move, together with the younger generation, to a new frontier.

Resistance may also come from a pastor. There are many reasons why a pastor may not see or heed signs of decline. We all have our blind spots. However, congregations that pretend to follow the leader, saying yes when they mean no, for example, only assist the pastor in delaying progress. In addition, it is fair to consider that your pastor's livelihood depends on the continuance of your ministry. Asking a pastor to weigh in on a decision about closure puts him or her in a difficult spot. S/he may want to hold on as long as possible, even if that is not the best decision for the church. Or your pastor may be frustrated enough to want a quick way out of the situation.

One night a couple of lay leaders and I attended yet another program about church revitalization. On the ride home, as we discussed the program, one of the women said, "Maybe we should think about closing the church." This possibility had been lurking among us for a decade, but finally, here was someone willing to speak of it out loud. I was caught off guard by her comment and felt I should not express an opinion one way or another. After a pregnant moment I said, "Well, that would be something we should talk to the regional minister about, not something we should decide on our own." Ours was a connectional polity system, so I knew that was protocol. More importantly, I felt it was important not to squelch the idea with false optimism by saying something like, "Oh no, we'll get through this rough spot somehow." I needed my lay leaders to hear they had my permission, as pastor and paid staff, to explore the idea of closure, if that was where they were being led.

When resistance breaks down and you sense that some members of your congregation are ready to discuss significant downsizing decisions, such as reducing down to a part-time pastor, selling your building, doing a merger, or closing the church altogether, it is best to widen the conversation to include your pastor, your regional judicatory leader, and/or an appropriate committee of the wider church.

Doing a prayerful, thoughtful assessment of the state of your church takes honesty and observation. It shifts the congregation from asking, "How do we fix our church?" to asking, "What is our church like now?" The assessment will not give you the magic next step to success. It will help you to know where you are, and how you got there. From there, you may be able to see God's next step on the path.

QUESTIONS FOR REFLECTION

But we have this treasure in clay jars, so that it may be made clear that this extraordinary power belongs to God and does not come from us.

2 CORINTHIANS 4:7

- What extraordinary power has God granted your congregation?
- Talk about the various roles of lay leaders in your congregation. Who is a spiritual leader? Matriarch or patriarch? Who are your resident experts? Who is an insightful outsider? Gather a group of active members and identify each person's spiritual gifts. How can you engage each person in the discernment process?
- What kinds of assessment and discernment tasks are already occurring, formally or informally, in your church now? What kinds of information still need to be gathered?

5

Discerning the Failure to Thrive: Pastors

Nobody taught us in seminary how to close a church.

Pastor Mark

During a decade of leading a struggling church, I sought out resources for assistance, but all I could find was advice about revitalization. I was sent to "transformation" conferences and stewardship events. I was invited to workshops on new models for Sunday School, planned giving representatives came by, and my regional pastor encouraged us to share our building with community groups, which we did. I learned new ways to foster spiritual formation and engage in community outreach. While some of these ideas were working fabulously for my colleagues, they were all geared toward churches that had an institutional future. Increasingly, I felt lost in the world.

When I heard the term "failure to thrive" described by a hospice social worker, it reminded me of something I was seeing in my church. Opportunities would come along for the church to take on a mission challenge or reach out to new neighbors. A financial gift would be given or a creative new person would come to worship. But for some reason, the church body did not welcome these opportunities in ways that caused them to be enlivened, to *thrive*.

While I observed these signs, I was reluctant to point them out to the membership. I expected them to notice what was happening on their own and change their behavior. What I didn't realize was that the average member cannot always see their behavior objectively, while the pastor sometimes can. It was up to me to gently share my perception of what was happening, even if my perception might not be received positively.

When I arrived at the church, my regional pastor had warned me: "We've done all we can for them." She told me they had received the assistance of grants and consultants but had not made good use of the outside assistance. Because of this trend, I was told not to expect any more help from the wider church. We were, in essence, "on our own."

While I heard and heeded her message, I still believed that, with the right kind of leadership, the church could not only survive, but thrive. I had to learn for myself what this church's limits were. I introduced new ideas, prompted the congregation to follow through on some of their ideas, and I "pinch hit" for them when they abandoned their commitments. I was advised to be their cheerleader, but I noticed their cheers were pretty faint. Eventually I discovered that, without the support of the wider church, and without the leadership of an overfunctioning pastor like myself, this church would probably be unable to maintain a healthy institutional life.

It took me a long time to learn to read the signs of "failure to thrive," and during that time I did a lot of blaming. Sometimes I blamed myself and questioned my own gifts for ministry. Other times, I blamed the congregation, whom I resented for their inability to "shape up." Now and then, I blamed the regional body for abandoning us.

In the final stage of my ministry at that church, it was a colleague who provided a pointed revelation for me that my congregation was losing its ability to function. During my sabbatical, I asked him to lead my governing board's monthly meeting. Upon my return, he told me how it went. "I noticed that they can't seem to make any decisions. They just table everything for later." The sirens flashed in my head when I heard that critique. On a subconscious level, I had been aware of this for a while. The congregation was losing its capacity to be self-determining. The anxiety and fear associated with their decline had frozen them up.

VITALITY VS. VIABILITY

We have been using the words *vitality* and *viability* because they describe two different ways of looking at organizational health. A *viable* church, by my definition, is one that has sufficient resources (financial and human) to maintain its current level of programming, staffing, and building maintenance without depleting financial resources such as endowments or the spiritual energy of the leadership. The active membership is equipped to perform basic ministry tasks. Its property is maintained on an up-to-date basis. It is able to keep up with denominational standards for paying the staff necessary to lead the congregation. These are objective standards for economic viability.

But a viable church is not necessarily a vital ministry, and not all vital churches are viable. *Vitality* describes a church's ability to accomplish its mission with vigor. A congregation may identify its core mission to be care for the poor in their immediate neighborhood, Christian education and faith formation, or advocating for justice issues. One church I know of has made spiritual nurture a focus, providing a labyrinth, holistic healing professionals, and retreat space for the wider community. Another church provides a free weekly meal to the neighborhood. Some churches attempt to provide a "full service" ministry that provides a little of everything to a diverse membership. Whatever its mission, a vital congregation is clear about stating it *and* has the resources to carry it out faithfully.

The sad truth at this time in history is that many congregations are lacking in vitality or viability. One regional leader I spoke with admitted to me that just under half of the churches he oversees are deficient in *both* areas. He drew a four-square chart and wrote the words "vital and viable" in one; in the next, he wrote "vital, but not viable." In the third square he wrote "viable, but not vital," and in the fourth, he wrote "not viable and not vital." He told me that a small number of churches in his district were vital and viable, healthy churches. Many of his churches were viable: paying the bills and maintaining basic ministry, but not what could be called vital. They were not reaching out and growing with creative new forms of ministry. He named two new church developments in his district that were vital, but not yet viable and self-sustaining financially. And finally he turned to the fourth quadrant: he confessed with sadness that the majority of his churches were neither vital nor viable.[1] These are the kind of churches I anticipate will be selling buildings, merging, or closing in the next decade.

How do pastors read the signs of lagging vitality and viability in ways that allow us to intervene either for revitalization, downsizing, merger, or completion of a ministry? Instead of thrashing a congregation with

---

1. This interviewee did not indicate how he had made his assessment of vitality and viability.

expectations about growth and renewal, when is it the right time to turn their hearts to a different kind of hope?

For the pastor of a declining church, the reading of signs may be just as difficult as it is for the laity. In our day-to-day management of our church families, we focus on the needs we were called to serve: weekly worship, counseling, administration, and teaching. There isn't much time to consider the "big picture" of the church's vitality and viability.

In my experience, I could usually shut out the "big picture" of where my church was headed until the fall of each year. Then, reality would seep in again. The nominating committee would wrestle with the same few names available to fill leadership positions. The stewardship and budget committees would stare at the church's lean books, searching for ways to trim expenses. The denomination would send a letter telling the congregation how much more they should pay me the following year in order to keep up with inflation. Someone would count the members lost to death or disappearance, and we would calculate our per capita offering to the wider church.

Every fall, we would muddle through somehow, and I would tell myself it was just the lot of the small church to be forever on the brink. But after a while, the dread got deeper, and I began to do the kind of objective data gathering I recommend to laity in chapter 4.

One time I made a chart graphing our membership gains and losses over the 45-year life of the church and showed it to our leaders. It displayed a robust upward surge in the early years, followed by a plateau, and then a rather alarming decline throughout the 1990s. My little flock looked at the chart, expressionless.

"What's wrong with them?" I asked my husband later. "Don't they care that we're losing members?"

"It's not that they don't care," he said thoughtfully. "It's that they don't know what to do with that information."

As the years progressed, the signs of decline became more clear and our efforts to stave it off seemed more futile. Yet in other ways, the congregation seemed to be getting stronger. We engaged in more outreach with the neighborhood and shared our building with another congregation to make ends meet. We were more intentional in prayer together. I felt that, if we sold the building, we might be able to generate fuel for a unique, continuing ministry. But I could not muster the courage to say that out loud. When I at last asked my regional pastor to come and say it for me, it was too little, too late.

Through all of this, I was trying to avoid the pastoral task of speaking the truth in love to my people. Part of my reluctance to face that truth was rooted in a sense of failure: what had I done wrong? How come I could not save my church?

I now realize that *I was not alone, it was not all my fault, and my church was not a failure.* I also realize now that, as a trusted pastor, I was in a good position to state the hard truth. The work of the pastor is to be a prophet; it is our job to tell our own truth in ways that foster broader and more honest conversation.

THE CRITICAL MOMENT

Clergy leaders may wonder, "Is there some *critical moment* in a church's decline, that 'point of no return' when it is too late to rebuild a ministry in its current shape? And if there is such a moment, how can we recognize it?"

There are significant turning points in a church's life cycle at which the conversation about the future needs to change. Sometimes, a crisis occurs when your church is forced to make a decision quickly, such as in the case of a natural disaster. But in many cases, the moment of decision is not so clear.

Because your church is a complex system, the critical moment of recognition will come for different people at different times. One by one, members will begin to recognize that the church as it once was no longer exists and new behavior is required of them. A few people may talk to each other or the pastor about these issues, without the overall behavior of the church showing any sign of change. Finally, a "tipping point" event will bring enough people to awareness of the situation that a shift in consciousness and behavior will take place. The tipping point may be a *moment of crisis*, such as a needed building repair that cannot be put off or the resignation of a leader.

But there are others types of "critical moments." One is a *moment of opportunity*. God may place an opportunity before the congregation, and the congregation must discern whether to respond or not.

St. James Church was offered an opportunity to function in a new way when a multicultural center approached them to share their downtown building. The church's pastor and presbytery pressed them to enter a shared building relationship, but the congregation resisted the new arrangement at every turn. An opportunity was lost and the church closed not long after.

In my own setting, God sent Rev. Lee to the church door one rainy day. He was looking for space for his small Hmong congregation to worship on Saturdays. We were able to enter an arrangement that not only offered us shared space, but also shared fellowship and education about Hmong culture. This was not a *critical moment* in the sense that it "saved" our church, but it was an opportunity that allowed both congregations to grow in their community connection and cultural understanding.

Yet another definition of a critical moment is a *kairos* moment. The Greek word *kairos* is often interpreted in the Bible as "the fullness of time." It is the moment that God puts in front of us for the right thing to happen at the right time. It is not our job to make that time happen; that's God's job. But it is our job to notice that the moment has arrived and to give ourselves to whatever God is doing to fulfill God's will in that moment. Some people believe that the decline of the institutional church as it exists today is occurring in a *kairos* time, in which we are being called to let go of the old models that grounded us and commit ourselves to new ways of being Christ's church in the future. Pastoral leaders can help their congregations discern the *kairos* they are living in by watching for signs of God's activity in their context and inviting people to respond to that activity in new ways.

In discerning what constitutes a *critical moment* in the life or decline of a church, leaders should look not only for danger signs, but for signs of opportunity to follow the Spirit into new connections and behaviors. God is constantly doing a new thing, and it is our job to be ready for God's surprising intervention.

WHY DO I HAVE TO SAY IT?

In the mid 1980s, toward the end of my mother's battle with cancer, her oncologist was presenting us with more invasive options to extend her life. He never told us her condition was "terminal." When, at the last, weakened by the ravages of chemotherapy treatments, her kidneys began to shut down, the doctor asked us to make a decision about dialysis.

Luckily, we had enough regard for my mother at that point that we rejected this treatment and allowed her to die peacefully. But it was up to our family to face the reality of her impending death. The doctor never said "It's time to say good-bye." Indeed, his only job, as he saw it, was to keep her body functioning.

Medicine has progressed since those days, and her case would probably be handled with more sensitivity today. Today, a good doctor would have referred her for hospice care. She would likely have died at home, peacefully surrounded by family and relieved of pain.

Recalling this experience reminds me that the pastoral leader, like a good doctor, is accountable to carefully read signs of decline and help the congregation begin the necessary conversation and discernment that will lead to significant change. There may be few, if any, lay members in the system who are willing to initiate this on their own.

Pastor Mark's church still had adequate funds to stay open for a few more years. When I asked him why he felt he needed to initiate these conversations before the money ran out, he pointed out the advanced age of most of his members and asked, "What will happen to the system once you step out, if you don't address the issues now? What messes are you leaving in the hands of frail members and overworked district pastors?"

Pastor Bob was a trained interim who was called in to assist a church that had all but concluded that they wanted to close before he got there. But before they proceeded with a closure process, he wanted to help them first consider whether they might still be expressing the mission and character of an authentic church. "Were we manifesting that for our community, or were we displaying a broken image of church to the community?" He asked his congregation to study *ecclesiology*, the primary functions of the church of Jesus Christ. After they engaged in the study, they looked at each other and concluded that they no longer had the energy to perform the basic tasks of a Christian community.

Pastor Karl was called to a church that his regional pastor had advised to close. The members wanted to stay open, but they were deeply divided by old conflicts. Karl and his regional pastor called each member into his office to talk with them about continuing the ministry. He asked each person why they wanted the church to stay open, what level of commitment he could expect from them if they continued, and whether they would be willing to put old conflicts aside for the good of the community. Many members, though not all, stated their willingness to put their differences aside for the future of the church.

Each of these pastoral leaders found ways to take responsibility for naming and addressing the issues of decline in their settings. While leaders do not always have the power to determine outcomes, they can use the power they have to do their own listening and assessment and then tell others what they perceive.

Toward the Better Country

WAYS TO START THE CONVERSATION

Over the years, I have tried to start meaningful conversations among small groups in churches, attempting to introduce some new idea at a leadership retreat, a governing board meeting, or a series of cottage meetings. In a healthy church, this sometimes works. But when I've tried this in a church experiencing anxiety, it did not go so well. In some groups, a few voices will dominate the conversation while others remain silent. In others, the group easily gets off course and lapses into chitchat. If there is uncomfortable business to discuss, many people would prefer to pick one or two trusted friends to talk to in the parking lot.

I once attended a webinar with Alice Mann in which she presented a conversation model that may work well in a small congregation. The pastor might start one-on-one conversations with key leaders. Sit down and say, "I'm wondering about our church's future options. . . ." and invite each person to discuss their perceptions of the church's ministry and future. Then give them a short article on the topic of church vitality and viability to read and go on to another person. After talking to a few people, the pastor might invite them all to get together and talk about the article and their thoughts. Then see if the group generates its own energy to widen the conversation. The object here is not to push your own agenda, but to begin a genuinely open conversation about the future.

Starting the conversation one on one is a way to prime the pump for addressing the more serious questions people may need to discuss:

- *Why are we not getting much spiritual energy from worship lately?*

- *Why it is that, no matter how much I give financially, it's never enough?*

- *I miss the people who don't come anymore.*

- *I miss the choir. I want to go to a church that has a choir.*

Some questions, like whether you can afford to pay the pastor, or whether the building is worth repairing, are taboo subjects that may only come up in one-on-one conversation.

Pastor Don has worked extensively with small, rural congregations, both as a pastor and as a consultant. He told me he often starts conversations in informal ways. Before and after worship, he hangs around and talks to people individually: "How do you feel things are going here at First Church? How is it different than it used to be? What kinds of things have you been doing to respond to those changes? How is that going for you? Have you ever considered. . . ?"

These types of questions allow church members to express themselves without judgment or being told "You should do this. . . ." Don's questions are a gentle invitation for his congregations to evaluate their ministry and challenge themselves to consider new options. Some people will just vent and complain. If so, he simply listens and moves on. But others will show some curiosity. "I wonder what that would be like. . . ." With these people, Pastor Don pursues conversation in depth. They are the kind of people who might dare to think and act creatively.

Once the conversation has been opened up, a leader may want to present a set of evaluative questions to members of the congregation and ask each person to reflect on the current state of the church. Allowing members to reflect individually and write answers down gives them time to think independently and allows for more introverted members to formulate their thoughts. Group reflection then allows each person to be heard, while also benefiting from the insights of others. In family systems theory, this is known as "self-differentiation."

Questions might include:

Self-Governance and Adaptation to Change

- Is your congregation able to govern itself without constant intervention from a pastor or regional leader?
- Do you have a responsive administrative structure that is appropriate to your church's size?
- Do you take advantage of opportunities for developing new ministries?
- Has the congregation displayed the ability to address and resolve church conflict in the recent past?

Spiritual Vitality

- What is the mood of worship like?
- Are worshipers experiencing spiritual growth and depth by association with the church? What kind of evidence supports your answer?
- Does the congregation include the presence of spiritually mature leaders and can you identify who they are?

Mission

- Can members articulate what your church's mission is?
- Is the church's mission relevant to some portion of the local community outside your membership, and if so, to whom?
- List some of your church's spiritual assets. How are you making use of these assets to fulfill your mission?

Financial Sustainability

- Account for all your sources of income. How will these sources change in the next three to five years?
- Make an accounting of your expenses, including the cost of maintaining your physical plant. Are there major repairs or other expenses looming on the horizon? What proportion of your income is being spent on pastoral leadership? Is there a realistic plan for funding these expenses over the next few years?

Pastor Bob, at Riverview Church, used a spiritual discernment process he discovered in a book by Beth Ann Gaede.[2] It began with small group conversation and widened to include the entire congregation over time. Some churches have tried Appreciative Inquiry resources to foster conversation, while others have tried "asset mapping," a process of discovering spiritual gifts in the congregation and community, as they discern God's will and direction.[3]

One way to *stifle* the conversation is to frame it as being about "whether we should stay open or close our doors." In my research, I've found several churches that discovered new ways to do ministry together because *doing ministry together was their goal*. I would encourage leaders to frame the conversation as true discernment of the best ways God wants you to move forward in ministry. That question will help those who wish to leave the system to find new locations to carry out their individual calls. And it will help those who stay together, or merge with another church, to focus on

2. Gaede, *Ending with Hope.*

3. Appreciative Inquiry and asset mapping are organizational and community development methods used in both church and secular settings. See Additional Resources in the back of the book.

pursuing a common mission, not just the institution's survival. In chapter 7, you will read about a few of the creative options churches have discovered to continue their ministry after an irreversible decline.

Whether you begin one-on-one, or with a more formal discernment process, these types of conversations must be brought to the surface, or a church is destined to die a slow death in shared silence. Once individuals' concerns are brought to the surface, the group can consider its options, listen to God together, and reclaim their power to move forward.

TEST THE DOMINANT VOICES

When Pastor Bob interviewed for his transitional pastorate at Riverview Church, the leadership "all looked at each other and said, 'Our goal is to figure out whether or not we should remain open as a congregation.' It was honestly one of the clearest goals I ever had from a church," he said. But Bob was not convinced that the church was ready to take this step. He took the position on the condition that he could do his own assessment of the situation. He talked with lay leaders separately and met with small groups. He fully expected that some members would come out of the woodwork and argue for the continuation of the church's ministry, perhaps in some new form. But to his surprise, after focused assessment, the message from members was unchanged: God was calling them to close their doors and give away their substantial legacy.

"My mentality originally was: they're going to have to prove to me that they need to close. I had that typical pastoral idea that the church should stay open at all costs." In retrospect, he says it was better for him and the church that they had to convince him of the rightness of their decision to close.

TRUST YOUR INSTINCTS

It is important to listen to the voices of people in the pews who have likely known this church longer and more deeply than you have. As Pastor Don says, "The members of the church have more skin in the game than the pastor." However, as a relative outsider, you and your regional pastor have a unique "balcony" perspective that should also be trusted.

Regional pastors may offer helpful insights about a congregation, especially if they have significant history in the region. I would advise pastors to listen to those insights carefully. A regional pastor has observed not only your congregation, but others like it, and may have insights that you and your congregation have missed. In some cases, however, a regional pastor may make inaccurate assumptions about a congregation simply because he or she cannot understand the complexities of each church the way its pastor can.

Pastor Mark was visited by a regional staff person who did a short assessment of the church involving half a dozen questions put to the leaders of the church. He reported to me that his church leaders "passed" the assessment with flying colors. The regional leader concluded her visit by telling them they should stay open and find a new mission project to engage in. This news hit Pastor Mark with "mixed emotions," since the church had already voted to close its doors the year before but was still looking for the wider church's blessing to do so.

For your part as pastor, you may be reluctant to admit to your regional body that your congregation is smaller and weaker than it appears on paper. Some congregations fear being "marked for closure" by their judicatory leaders and will hide their circumstances for as long as possible. The pastor's judgment of a situation can sometimes be clouded by emotions and fears. Several pastors expressed to me their discomfort with being the pastor who closed a church, because it seemed to mark them as a "professional risk." The best situation is when a pastor and denominational leader can openly discuss the welfare of the congregation without allowing honesty to "blacklist" a struggling pastor or congregation.

AVOID ASSUMPTIONS AND REFLECT ON BEHAVIOR

Pastoral leaders can be swayed to quick judgment about the direction a church should take if they listen too attentively to the dominant voices around them. Strong lay leaders, distant regional pastors, or colleagues may push a pastor in the wrong direction out of anxiety. If assessment of your church's current condition is not done carefully, and by a broad representation of members, staff, and regional leaders, inaccurate assumptions may be made about a church's vitality or lack thereof.

Not long ago, a colleague who knew about my research on church closure whispered to me his assumption that a certain church he knew of was so small, it must be on the brink of closure. It just so happened that I was scheduled to be that church's guest preacher in the near future, so I went with eyes open for signs of impending death. Instead, I was surprised to find a lively, vital congregation of about 35 worshippers. Of course, that didn't count the 12 puppets that were given front row seats in the sanctuary, a sign of the church's active puppet ministry. Downstairs, the tiny basement was loaded with stacks of neatly folded clothing. I learned that this congregation hosted the community's clothing bank and had teamed up with a nearby food pantry to provide supportive services to the rural poor in their community. Members cheerfully guided me through the service, a teenage girl collected the offering, and a funny cartoon elicited laughter as it was displayed on their simple projection equipment. It didn't matter that the church was very small in membership. It appeared to be alive with the Holy Spirit.

One way of assessing the health of your congregation is to experiment with a change that might add vitality and see what happens. How does your governing board and congregation respond to experiments and risks? If they respond in healthy ways (e.g., with humor, curiosity, or lively conversation), let them know they are capable of more change. If they respond negatively (arguing, secretiveness, stonewalling), let them know what you observe. A church incapable of even small changes in the midst of decline is a church that should be planning for an orderly closure.

Finally, reach out for collegial support from a trusted colleague or clergy group. The maze of doing healthy discernment in the midst of anxiety is enough to drive any good leader a little crazy. We are tempted to cling to the wrong saviors at such a time. When I sensed that my judgment about my pastorate was compromised by stress, I sought out the help of a spiritual director, with whom I met once a month for the last year of my ministry. This person's job was to hear my stories, give feedback on my actions, and test my assumptions. She also prayed for me. Because of the grief and stress of watching my church die, I could not have made good leadership decisions without her assistance.

If the congregation is still able to employ you as a trained pastor, they are in a much better position to experience a healthy closure with your help. You have the tools of theological reflection, data gathering, wider church relationships, and administrative skills to assist with what may be one of the most challenging projects a congregation will get through. You are also in a good position to identify key spiritual leaders in the congregation who garner respect from the membership and will be useful in setting a course others can trust enough to follow.

Many churches in the last stages of their life do not have adequate pastoral care. Those who do are at a distinct advantage, as long as the pastor has the courage to assist them in discernment for the future. You are the best person to balance pastoral care with prophetic witness. You can engender trust that is probably not afforded to your judicatory leader. And you know better than anyone the specific gifts and needs of members who may need to move on to other churches. Do not underestimate the power of your presence or the importance of your ministry to a church that is considering closure.

WHEN SHOULD YOU STOP TALKING AND START LISTENING?

In my experience with a declining church, I found myself doing a lot of pushing. For some years, I was pushing them to work harder and grow their ministry. When that effort failed, I found myself pushing them to accept their losses and downsize. At a certain point, through the wise counsel of mentors, I realized I had to stop saving them from the pain of loss, and let the congregation address its own demise. When I stopped pushing, their feelings began to surface. Emotions expressed included denial, then anger at me (their leader), then depression. For a while, there was just a lot of silence.

One evening at a meeting, something happened that had never happened before. Someone said, "I remember when we would have maybe ten kids in Sunday School. That was fun." Everyone was quiet for a minute. I had the good sense to keep my mouth shut. Then, a couple others also talked about something they remembered. This was not a nostalgic kind of remembering. It was an honest acknowledgment by the lay leaders that things were now different than they once had been. Acceptance of their current situation was beginning to sink in. It was not something I could push them into.

In the anxiety of dealing with change, you will see a side of your congregation that perhaps you wish you didn't have to see. Different members will grieve in different ways, just like in a family. Some will withdraw, while others hover over insignificant details. Some will persist in carrying out old traditions, no matter how impractical, while others will want to grasp onto every shiny new program that comes in the mail. If we based our opinions of others on how they react to crises, it would be difficult to love anyone. Be gentle with your fellow Christians at this time of discernment. Try to love your church through its dark days and see whether that effort results in a congregation more firmly bound to one another and Christ. Whether your ministry continues in its current form, or a new form God is preparing you for, continue to stay open to the wisdom of the Holy Spirit and other believers who share your love for your church. The way of Christ is not always predictable; there may still be surprises and adventures to come for your congregation!

REFLECTION

O Jerusalem, Jerusalem, you who kill the prophets and stone those sent to you, how often I have longed to gather your children together, as a hen gathers her chicks under her wings, but you were not willing.

MATTHEW 23:37 (NRSV)

- Pastors sometimes feel that they are trying to tell the truth, but no one is listening. Other times, they feel they cannot tell the truth, or they will be "run out of town." If you could say something to your congregation that they would take to heart at this time in their life cycle, what would you say? Write it down in the form of a pastoral letter.

- Consider the roles of different leaders in your setting, including the pastor's and regional pastor's roles. Who has initiated or stifled conversation about your future? Who is your congregation most likely to turn to for wisdom?

- Identify any critical moments you have discerned recently. Were they moments of decision, moments of opportunity, or *kairos* moments? How have you and your congregation responded to these moments in the past?

6

Discerning the Failure to Thrive:
Regional Pastors

"Come, go down to the potter's house, and there I will let you hear my words." So I went down to the potter's house, and there he was working at his wheel. The vessel he was making of clay was spoiled in the potter's hand, and he reworked it into another vessel, as seemed good to him. Then the word of the Lord came to me: Can I not do with you, O house of Israel, just as this potter has done? says the Lord. Just like the clay in the potter's hand, so are you in my hand, O house of Israel."

JEREMIAH 18:1–6 (NRSV)

DURING A BREAK AT a wider church meeting, I looked over at my colleague Warren, a regional pastor, who was pensively fingering his day calendar. On the calendar were neatly written appointments on just about every day. "Busy week?" I asked him. He sighed. "Since my region has cut staff, I'm starting to cover twice the area I used to cover. That means twice as many meetings. Twice as many churches."

The decline in participation in local churches has translated into a dramatic decrease in funding for wider church ministries. Middle judicatory leaders are working harder and traveling farther to stay connected to their regions. Clergy at this level see all the worst-case scenarios: the high conflict, the clergy sexual abuse case, and the sudden heart attack in the pulpit. They struggle mightily to offer resources that will help churches maintain their voice in the community.

To be called upon to assist a church in planning a closure must seem a thankless task to the average denominational leader. The intervention may spark anger between the congregation and its judicatory. There will be uncomfortable meetings involving tears. And then there is the self-doubt that comes with a church closure: could the wider church have done anything differently to prevent it?

WHAT IS YOUR ATTITUDE ABOUT CLOSURE?

In interviews with regional leaders, I encountered three basic attitudes about church decline and closures:

1. Sadness: Stuart is a regional leader of his judicatory who became emotional when I told him about my research. He then told the story of the one tiny church he had helped close years before, and the many churches in his region that would likely face closure in the next ten years. The reality of church closures was, to him, a symbol of all the loss the church is experiencing in this new century, and his grief was raw.

2. Cynicism: "I've never seen a closure go well," said Loretta, a regional leader. She had been on the front lines in dealing with a number of conflicted small churches, two of which had closed. Because of her experience, she associated all closures with high conflict.

3. Hopeful stoicism: a denominational leader who served at the national level remarked, "All the churches the Apostle Paul started have since closed."

My colleague Warren reflected on the issue of closure this way: "It's God's Church and God will do a new thing. It may not look like it does now. But I trust God to continue on. Those are the eyes of faith. It will be what it'll be. It's okay. God will take care of us."

If you are a regional pastor, consider the attitude you bring to churches in decline. Do you feel sorry for them or think they have failed? Do they make you angry or remind you of your own weaknesses? What does resurrection mean in their situations? Your attitude will be apparent in the way you relate to churches at risk of closure.

WHY DO YOU HAVE TO SAY IT?

My interviews with middle judicatory pastors from various denominations gave me the sense that these leaders are wary of intervening in the discernment process of churches experiencing deep decline, even when their polity allows them to do so. While every denomination has its own process for guiding a church through institutional change, the common fear among those I talked to was that their congregations might become angry and defensive if the wider church intervened in ways that were insensitive or too directive.

Perhaps some of the reticence they feel has been sparked by the behavior of the Roman Catholic Church over the last several decades, as one diocese after another has engaged in massive church consolidation. There is widespread feeling that the Roman Catholic strategy of church closings has been heavy-handed and insensitive to the pastoral needs of the communities affected, many of them in poor, urban, or rural neighborhoods. Parish members were not included in the discernment process, and sufficient time was not allowed for members to grieve their losses and establish new ties with neighboring parishes.[1] In addition, the financial management of church property and assets by various dioceses has been held in question.[2]

But mainline and evangelical traditions have their own quagmire to wade through when considering who controls the life and death of congregations and the assets they hold. And anxious behavior can occur on the part of local churches, too.

Pastor Dan at Zion United Methodist Church told of an attempt made by the previous pastor to sell some of the church's real estate "under the radar" in order to generate operating funds. In this case, knowing they needed permission from their district superintendent for such an action, lay members stopped the pastor from proceeding with a sale.

In another story told to me, a Lutheran (ELCA) congregation was pressured by the synod to hold a hasty congregational vote to close their church and was told to vacate its property. Instead, a group of members resisted the synod's demand and procured a high-risk mortgage in order to continue meeting their operating expenses. The synod changed the locks to prevent them from entering the building. A lengthy legal battle has taken this case all the way to its state's Supreme Court, but the congregation has

1. Gaede, *Ending With Hope*, 4.
2. The Economist, "Earthly Concerns," para. 1.

continued to lose the fight against the synod.[3] In matters of control over the future of beloved churches, there is room for error on the part of every stakeholder.

ASSET OR LIABILITY?

The question of who controls a church and its assets in the case of closure has led to legal battles between denominations and their own local churches. This issue is complicated by the fact that some church assets are not as desirable as others. A large, city-center property may be valued in the six- or seven-figure range, while a congregation with the same number of worshippers in a tiny clapboard rural church may be a liability when it needs to be torn down. Financial assets that can be converted into new mission resources are coveted by the wider church. Buildings in decay and endowments with many strings attached to their use are considered "white elephants."

As a wider church leader, regardless of your power and polity, you may find yourself struggling to balance your respect for healthy congregational self-determination with a desire to avoid the future burden of abandoned souls and properties.

In the healthiest closures I studied, congregations were allowed to be somewhat self-determining about how church assets were used or distributed. Whether episcopal, connectional, or congregational, local and wider church leaders communicated regularly and cooperated in decision making together. The wider church respected the local church's input regarding how its legacies might be redistributed, and the local church honored its denomination's interest in wise stewardship that uses assets to fund future ministry ventures. If there is no mutual dialogue and shared decision making about the stewardship of assets, there may be lingering suspicion about how "the presbytery/conference/synod stole our church."

With emotions and financial assets at stake, it is natural for leaders to avoid conflict. One frustrated transitional pastor told me, "Everyone assumes another level of the church is in charge." Even as regional leaders told me they felt intervention in a struggling church should occur sooner for a better outcome, most admitted that they generally "wait for a crisis" before stepping in.

3. 2X2 Virtual Church, "SEPA/Redeemer."

Unfortunately, waiting for a crisis just about assures us that church closures will occur in a climate of crisis. So, what kind of intervention might be possible? With the limited energy regional leaders have to assist churches in discernment and transitions, there are a number of beneficial actions to consider that a regional leader may be in the best position to assist with.

CONSIDER WHO'S IN CHARGE

What does your denominational polity say about the relationship between a local congregation and its regional body? While your relationship with thriving congregations may seem clear, it's possible that your relationship with an at-risk congregation may necessarily need to change.

Keith, an executive presbyter (EP), was asked how he decides to intervene. "Well first, how do you know intervention is needed ?" he asked. He says he may hear comments from pastors or lay leaders such as, "I wonder if we'll be able to stay open." Then he uses those opportunities to invite himself into a conversation with the governing board.

"They're usually very willing to have me come. But when I get there, I usually find, 'Oh, you just want our building, or you just want our money,' that approach. I spend a lot of time saying that's not what I'm here for. Let's look at the ministry here; look at who, how, why, and where we can go with what we have. It takes several meetings to have that conversation."

Loretta, another EP, expressed exasperation at declining churches that reach out for help. "They basically want enough money to maintain what they have. They will not say, 'We want to close,' but 'We don't know what to do.' They're like a teenager saying 'I hate you, I hate you, I hate you. Could you take me to the mall and give me $100?'"

In denominations that practice congregational autonomy, regional leaders expressed to me their frustration with the limits placed on them regarding how and when to intervene in at-risk churches. For example, UCC polity offers no formal point of entry into a local church's closure process until a decision for dissolution has been made. While local churches enjoy autonomy in determining their future, they have no wider church body that is obligated to be present at their deathbed vigils.

In his region, Warren, who is UCC, advocates for moving cautiously with intervention in a church at risk. He suggests that a judicatory leader must find his or her own right place in the continuum of leadership styles that might assist a church at the end of its life. A leader may be so hands-off she doesn't even know what is happening in the congregation until it is too late. Or he may be so directive he pushes a congregation into distrust of the wider church. Finessing the best timing and telling the truth in love, while offering realistic options to the congregation, is what Warren advises. His approach is to contact at-risk churches once a year or so to "check in" and invite more conversation if they want it.

STARTING THE CONVERSATION

Start by listening to the clergy and lay leaders, and let them describe their experience. Recall the gentle questions of Pastor Don in chapter 5, who asked members, "How do you feel things are going here at First Church? How is it different than it used to be? What kinds of things have you been doing to respond to those changes?" These questions invite the congregation to express its grief before being led forward.

Warren draws on his pastoral skills with struggling churches by encouraging their lay leaders. "Encourage them to work on personal spiritual growth to regain some sense of calm, enough to be able to consider their options. A church like this may not be able to think about grand visions of deeper discipleship. But maybe they can consider practical options for the short term, like sharing ministry resources with another church to balance their budget and extend their life."

Instead of rushing in with a plan and an answer, no matter how much the congregation may plead for one, invite them to talk with each other, their pastor, or a consultant. For all you know, God's plan may be unfolding among them and may just need to be uncovered.

GET HELP

Don't try to handle the pressure of church closure alone. Use your partners in the wider church to intervene before a church reaches a crisis stage. In Presbyterian and United Methodist polity, a congregation ordinarily cooperates with an appointed team of lay and clergy from neighboring churches when a significant discernment process is begun. These kinds of teams express the church's belief that all local churches are part of the one universal church and are accountable to one another as well as God. Because congregational polities have less built-in support structures, local churches may not reach out for help until all the healthy options for their future have disappeared. Look beyond your own limited schedule to locate others in your regional body who may be able to assist with supportive peer relationships, such as a Church and Ministry Division (UCC), a consultant, or a specially appointed discernment team. There is such a thing as having too much autonomy. If a congregation seems stuck or resistant to movement, consider forming a partnership between the pastor and a regional staff person or consultant to meet with the congregation's leaders, adding muscle to your message.

Some regional bodies have developed procedures and funding to assist at-risk congregations with discernment and transitional periods. One presbytery I interviewed offers 50/50 matching funding to any church in discernment about its future that hires a qualified church consultant. The Disciples of Christ have developed an assessment process called "New Beginnings" that brings in a trained consultant for two intensive days of work with a local congregation. Churches with episcopal-style polities can do discernment on a regional scale by using the services of Partners for Sacred Places, an organization that helps judicatories decide which churches should stay open and which should enter into consolidations. These types of programs give regional leaders help addressing the needs of struggling churches with limited staff time. They also challenge churches to invest with attention and dollars in intentional discernment about their futures.

It is wise to make neighbor churches aware of the concerns of the distressed church and to ask for their support. When Pastor Bob arrived at Riverview Church, his regional pastor connected him to two nearby pastors of the same denomination. Each of those pastors served as a support as he walked the congregation through discernment. When the closure finally occurred, most of the members chose to affiliate with one of those two neighbor churches, bringing assets from the church with them.

Seek out colleagues who have walked churches through closure. And remember that your pastoral skills may be more important than your knowledge of polity in dealing with a stressed or grieving congregation.

PASTORAL CARE AND PROPHETIC WITNESS

Warren describes some churches in steep decline as being "in survival mode." This type of church is "highly anxious; they can't be creative or rational anymore, and they're not even aware of it themselves. They can't make good choices anymore."

Gary described one of his churches as being "relieved" when he presented the option of closure to them, while another just seemed resigned to it. Loretta told me all the closures she had ever heard of were fraught with high conflict. How does a regional leader identify the land mines of grief in at-risk churches?

PROVIDE ADEQUATE RESOURCES

Your denomination's procedural guidelines may not include details as to how churches should engage in discernment that leads to downsizing, merger, or closure. It will be up to you to offer the congregation and its pastor a package of resources to begin with. Invite them to read this book together, and encourage the congregation to engage in community research, spiritual exercises, and assessment of the church's current health before proceeding with ideas for moving forward. Encourage them to explore all their options, and be open to the Holy Spirit's power. If *you* are open, maybe they will be, too. That Spirit may not "save" their church in its current form, but it may guide them into a new kind of life.

See chapter 7 to learn about more creative options churches have chosen when they were at risk of closing their doors. You will be amazed at the creative ministries a congregation can accomplish, working with the Spirit's inspiration. But among those options, name closure out loud as one, and let them know they will receive the blessing of the wider church if closure is the option God leads them to.

OFFER QUALITY PASTORAL LEADERSHIP

One of the best indicators of a healthy closure in the churches I interviewed was the availability of a competent pastor. The effective pastoral leaders I encountered had both hearts for pastoral care and the steel stomach for emotional decision-making opportunities. Special training in closure techniques was not available to any of these people. What they employed was a balanced passion for pastoral care to those letting go of the past and a sincere, prophetic vision of the *better country* God is leading us to.

If you can, offer at-risk congregations a suitable transitional pastor to guide them through their discernment process. In some cases, a settled pastor may be too tightly fused with the congregation to lead them in significant change. In other cases, a long-time pastor who has inspired trust will be the best person to offer pastoral care in a church's time of grief and loss. As regional staff, you may need to offer guidance about the kind of leadership needed in the transition, even if it means asking a settled pastor to resign.

Some churches are so small they cannot afford regular pastoral care, and they may be functioning with pulpit supply or a lay leader from the congregation. While such an arrangement may work well for a stable congregation, a church dealing with significant change needs leadership. Possibilities might include a lay pastor from the area who has training in pastoral care or facilitation, a consultant or retired pastor who will preach and take on additional duties of a discernment process, or a denominational group, such as a UCC Church and Ministry Committee.

TELL THE TRUTH IN LOVE

It is always difficult to be the bearer of bad news, but some churches need your outside authority to tell the truth. While you may be hesitant to hurt the feelings of fragile members, part of your role is to be a steward of God's gifts in sharing the Gospel of Jesus Christ. If you feel a local church is no longer fulfilling its mission, or a settled pastor needs to step aside, you may be the only one with the courage and voice to say this out loud.

Gary, an EP who has been involved in both rural and urban church closures, told of one case in which a downtown church was declining for twenty-five years. The long-time pastor kept saying, "When a few of the older members die, this church will be able to grow again." Finally, Gary gave the pastor a deadline for action. "You can't just close and give the building to the Presbytery," he said. "When your cash reserves get down to $10,000, you need to dissolve." In that case, the congregation and wider church worked together to prepare the building for sale to another congregation. The income generated from the sale was converted into a fund for church vitality projects and is now helping other fragile churches to be proactive about their futures.

HELP CHURCHES BE ACCOUNTABLE

If a church makes a decision for merger, closure, or the sale of their building, it is your job to provide them with the necessary steps to take, including tasks such as facilitating merger negotiations, authorization by a regional body to close or merge, dissolution of a nonprofit organization, and appropriate transfers of property deeds. While the local church may perform these duties itself, they will need your guidance, and that of an attorney, to complete them. When a final service is celebrated, you will be needed to lead a ritual that honors the church's historic mission and the ways they have chosen to carry that mission forward in new ways.

SHOW COMPASSION AND GRATITUDE

June was the moderator of her church when it closed and told, with deep emotion in her voice, of the many hours she spent in meetings and handling financial and property details at her former church. When she was through, I asked her if anyone among her denominational leaders and pastors had thanked her for her effort. She sat silently for a long time, and finally said, "No, not really."

Pastor Dan, a United Methodist, told me how much he appreciated the formal service of recognition that was held at his conference's annual meeting to honor the history of his church and all its former members after it closed. This form of grateful remembrance helped him make peace with the difficult process of closing his church.

Most judicatories have a system for regularly honoring retired clergy. It is appropriate also to recognize the gifts of churches that are nearing or have ended their ministry. Personally thank their pastor and lay leaders for their ministry. A congregation in decline is probably experiencing a sense of shame or low self-esteem. Remind them of the faithful ministry they have done. Find a way to publicly thank them. Through your position as a regional leader, you can convey hope and confidence in God's church to reshape itself for a new time. Congregations need to hear from their leaders that they are not alone, it is not all their fault, and their churches are not failures because they have declined or closed. They need your broader view of the challenges facing churches today, and they need to believe there is hope for the future.

Finally, when congregations express their grief about the decline of their churches, remind them of the hope of resurrection: Jesus did not return to us as the same man who died. He returned as the risen Christ. The church, too, will rise from the ashes of this time, in ways we cannot begin to imagine. Let your churches know you still rest in that hope.

REFLECTION

And [God] said to me, "You are my servant, Israel,
in whom I will be glorified."
But I said, "I have labored in vain,
I have spent my strength for nothing and vanity;
yet surely my cause is with the Lord,
and my reward with my God."

Isaiah 49:1–4 (NRSV)

- Judicatory leaders who oversee churches in various states of difficulty sometimes become cynical. What helps you to maintain hope in the face of church conflict and grief? How do you convey that hope to congregations and their pastors?

- In churches at risk of closure that you know of in your area, where do you see an entry point for conversation that helps them explore their options for the future?

7

Multiple Paths to the Future

When you have two choices, take the third.

Zen koan

IMAGINE YOURSELF WALKING IN the woods and becoming lost. You come to a place where your path forks off in two directions and you must make a choice. Which path will lead you home? You check for the direction of the sun, peer into the distance as far as you can, choose a path, and start walking. If it turns out to be a dead end, or you feel you are moving in the wrong direction, you may have to return to the fork and try the other path.

Now imagine there is no path at all. You will have to study the terrain with more attention: Where is brush blocking your way? Where can you get a steady foothold? In what direction might you find a clearing where you can get your bearings again? You will need to take one step at a time. Each step is a little investment in the future with no clear assurance of the outcome. The journey will take longer, and greater trust will be required.

Now imagine that someone is following you, counting on you to lead the way.

This is the situation many church leaders, lay and clergy, are experiencing in declining churches. We are making our way in new terrain, and even our pastors and regional leaders may feel ill-equipped to get us out of the woods unscathed. Congregations are used to having marked paths, traditions, and guidance with major transitions, but in a time of accelerating change, each congregation must be a pioneer on its own journey.

In your anxiety, you may see only one dark path ahead. With creativity and healthy discernment, you will discover there are many possible paths, and more than one way out of the woods. This chapter will explore some of the options churches have pursued in an effort to radically change, strengthen, or lengthen their ministry lives. These stories are meant to inspire your congregation to seek out its own unique path.

WHAT KIND OF CHANGE IS NEEDED?

As you consider all the options for your church's future, you will need to consider two types of change: technical change and adaptive change.[1] Technical changes are changes made to solve problems for which you know what the solution is. For example, if the sanctuary is full, you can add a second worship service. If giving goes down, you can cut staff hours, and so on. Your church has already made many technical changes in its ministry through the years, and more will be needed. Technical change builds on the solid foundation of your historic mission by making a few repairs to its framework.

Adaptive change is needed when your assumptions about your ministry and mission are called into question, and there is no quick fix for the problems you face. Here, the change occurs not so much in the institution, but in the hearts and minds of members. For example, many churches have found that attracting people to Sunday worship is no longer an easy task, no matter how wonderful the music and preaching. Renewed attention must be given to our ability to articulate and share our faith one on one with people *outside* the church if we want to grow disciples. We will need to become evangelists. Adaptive change means opening ourselves to be transformed from the inside out.

REVITALIZE, RIGHT SIZE, RELOCATE, OR RELINQUISH?

The overwhelming temptation for many churches is to "stay the same" for as long as possible. But staying the same should *not* be an option on the

---

1. The terms "adaptive change" and "technical change" were coined by Ron Heifetz and Marty Linsky in the book *Leadership on the Line*.

table. In every church, change is coming whether you plan for it or not. In churches rapidly declining in size or energy, that change will be significant. The question is *not*: what kind of change do you want? The question is: what kind of change does God want for you? After eliminating the temptation to do nothing, your congregation may seek God's direction to:

- *Revitalize* your ministry in its current form,
- *Right-size* your ministry to help the mission become more vital and viable,
- *Relocate* your mission through a building sale, a merger, or nesting in another church, or
- *Relinquish* your mission to God's control and disband your congregation.

Let's clarify the difference between these approaches.

REVITALIZATION

Much has been written about how churches can be revitalized by both technical and adaptive change. In order to revitalize its ministry, a congregation may discern and follow a completely new mission strategy or engage in some other form of adaptive change.

For example, Peace Church redirected its more traditional ministry toward a new, intentional outreach to the unchurched. They started by updating their building and adding contemporary worship (these might be considered "technical changes"). A few years later, they began focusing on each member's spiritual gifts and were led to engage in deeper, adaptive change, as individual members pursued spiritual growth and discipleship in small groups. A new structure evolved, which included forming task groups that carry out small group ministries such as community gardening, a summer youth program, a drama group, and free Saturday morning breakfasts for the neighborhood. The same pastor and many of the same members stayed with the congregation throughout these changes, which spanned more than a decade. The congregation's membership numbers have stayed stable, but the members have grown spiritually and proved to be remarkably resilient as their character and mission were transformed. This revitalization required openness to both technical and adaptive changes that were mission-driven, along with a team that included an energetic pastor and committed lay leaders.

Churches that are willing to engage in serious revitalization efforts are sometimes successful in creating more vital, viable congregations, but the effort and change required will be considerable. If you think your church has a chance of experiencing this kind of renewal, you should explore this option.

- Does your congregation have energy, courage, creativity, and the financial means for comprehensive change?

- Can you enlist the kind of pastoral leader who will commit to several years of deep discernment and transformation?

- Are you located in a growing community?

- Are you willing to give up "sacred cows" such as your ethnic identity or your favorite music in order to invite a different cultural or age group into ministry?

If the answer to these questions is yes, you may be what some call a "turnaround church." There are many resources, consultants, and denominational programs that can help you plan for radical transformation that will attract younger Christians, new immigrant groups, or the unchurched.

RIGHT-SIZING

Some churches can no longer be identified as "turnaround churches," but they are not ready to "close up shop." These churches are doing healthy ministry but are struggling with the cost of doing business at a smaller size (they still have vitality but are not viable). These churches may want to pursue a strategy of "right-sizing" their ministry for more focus on a particular mission.

First, remember that it is okay to be small! In their work as church consultants, Presbyterian pastors Linda Kuhn and Dave King have identified assets of the smaller congregation that make it an efficient agent of ministry, in a world where "bigger is not always better." They write,

> Healthy small churches have distinct advantages in this age of post Christendom: They can communicate rapidly and effectively; their relationships are deep and strong; they can be nimble in response to changing circumstances; they have a rich experience of trusting God to lead and support them in difficult times; they know and understand the resources (even if limited) that God has placed at their disposal; they often have a history of strong lay leadership; and, they tend to act without waiting for permission if the need requires.[2]

2. King, "Smaller for a Purpose," para. 3.

However, if your church used to be twice the size it is now, you will need to learn to function in new ways. A new size of church requires a new mission strategy, and perhaps a new mission. A congregation may gain focus and energy by doing the kind of honest assessment outlined in chapters 4 and 5 and listening to where God is leading you at your new size.

Technical changes to right-size your church may include:

- Staffing pattern (do you still need a custodian 20 hours per week?)
- Building use needs (can you rent out the Sunday school wing to a private school?)
- Structure (do you still need ten committees to run a church with a hundred active members?)

Adaptive changes might include:

- Redefining your mission: instead of the smorgasbord of mission projects you once supported only with dollars, study your neighborhood and your church's assets and use the gifts you find to develop a unique mission that you can address with hands-on volunteer help (for example, tutoring school children or housing a "memory café" for the elderly[3])
- Engage in leadership training that will transform your church into a lay-led mission organization. With stronger lay leadership, pastoral staff may be employed part-time or shared with another congregation.
- Offer education and spiritual formation beyond the church walls to learners in the community or at members' workplaces; give as much attention to people outside your membership as you do to those inside your walls.
- Promote use of your building by community nonprofit organizations and partner with them in shared mission ventures.

In a time of rapid change, resizing your church is an adaptive strategy that seeks to continue a vital ministry at a scale that fits your context and increases its viability. Remember, vitality and viability require having the financial, human, and organizational power to carry out a significant mission. You should be clear about why the mission needs to be performed and who will perform it. Keeping the doors open for your existing members is not a mission that can lead your congregation toward either numerical or spiritual growth. Following are a few more ideas for technical or adaptive changes that may increase your church's vitality and viability.

3. A "Memory Café" is a community gathering place for people with dementia and their caregivers. See Additional Resources for information.

PROGRAM CHANGES

Face the fact that some programs you accomplished in the past may no longer be feasible. Instead of doing nothing, update an old program for a new mission purpose. For example, a waning women's fellowship program might be disbanded, and those same members could be engaged in a new outreach to at-risk children through the schools.

When I arrived at a church in steep decline, there was no functioning Sunday school. We instituted a one-room school house using a workshop rotation model. Four adults each taught once a month. One week, Abraham and Sarah might arrive as storytellers. The next week, the children might cook recipes from the Bible. Gradually, families came to trust that some form of education would be provided for their children each week, with various ages learning together. My own daughter received a good Christian education in this way, and she enjoyed relationships with several "grand-mas" and "uncles" who knew her intimately. This congregation had to give up its old ideas about how to carry out Christian education and invent a new way of accomplishing the task.

The actual programming chosen will be unique in each situation. As with any other effort toward greater vitality, the focus should not be on "surviving a little longer," but on pursuing a common mission and making changes that assist the congregation to fulfill that mission more effectively.

STAFFING

One of the earliest signs that a church is losing viability is when it feels forced to move from a full-time to a part-time salary package. The cost of employing a full-time pastor has risen over the years due to health insurance and other factors. This, along with lower overall giving to churches by a smaller cadre of members, adds up to greater financial stress on churches. A rule of thumb in recent years is that it takes an average of at least 100 worshipers each Sunday to sustain a full-time pastor and basic programming.

And yet, the historic church has existed over many centuries without full-time professional clergy, and many small churches have existed without full-time staffing for decades. A congregation that is open to adaptive change may be able to continue vital ministry with part-time pastoral care.

Some denominations, such as the United Methodist Church, attempt to provide full-time employment for all clergy by creating yokes of parishes within geographical areas. Others will allow a congregation to create a part-time pastorate based on a percentage of the recommended full-time salary package. It is up to the pastor and governing board to determine what constitutes the part-time expectation. For example, how many hours or days per week will you work? How many vacation days will you accrue? Will the congregation provide full health, housing, and pension benefits? And what programs will be led by lay leaders because of the part-time arrangement?

One model of shared pastoral leadership involves a cluster of small churches, each with a trained lay preacher. Philip Hughes, who studied this model in the Uniting Church of Australia, explains how lay leaders team with ordained leaders to provide staffing:

> South Australia is sparsely populated agricultural country. Small towns, many with Uniting Churches, serve the communities. Only a few of these churches have their own ordained minister. Most ministers serve a cluster of three or more churches, often assisted by lay teams, which take some services. Many churches are led by teams of lay people.

While some American church leaders might be concerned about the quality of lay leadership, Hughes's research concluded that "the vitality of the lay-led churches was no different from churches led by ordained ministers. In many lay-led churches there is a strong sense of ownership by the lay people, and those involved in leadership often reported that they had grown in faith through their responsibilities."[4]

In some denominations, trained lay pastors are now being permanently installed in small church settings. There are pros and cons to this arrangement. Many lay pastors bring valuable life experience and training to ministry. However, it is not to be assumed that, just because your church is small, it is easy to lead. Sending an inexperienced leader into a church full of land mines, or asking a member with light training to assume pastoral duties in his or her own church, may be extremely stressful for the leader and create more problems than it solves.

The availability of lay pastors is unpredictable, depending on where you live. One denominational leader, Keith, told me that in the urban area he oversees, he has access to many ordained clergy who are willing to work in part-time ministry. But in his outlying, rural areas, he calls on lay pastors more often to fill part-time calls.

4. Hughes, "Lay Leadership in Sparsely Populated Rural Australia," abstract.

If your congregation is very small, you may try hiring supply pastors or visiting preachers who fill the pulpit on Sundays and perhaps moderate your governing board meetings. Visiting preachers can offer a variety of styles to complement a strong, lay-led congregation. However, keep in mind that a supply pastor is not a congregational leader. His or her function is to provide a worship experience only. A leader may still be needed to help guide your congregation in its discernment about the future. You might consider hiring a church consultant or a trained transitional pastor, or working with a denominational representative to help you discern God's direction in making significant decisions.

Your pastor may not be your only staff member, but he or she is your most expensive employee. That's why I believe it is beneficial for small churches to hire part-time staff (or appoint qualified volunteers) to assist with duties that may drain the pastor's time away from important ministry tasks. A secretary can be hired for an affordable salary to type and print bulletins, maintain a website, and print newsletters. A paid music leader, offering a few hours per week, can bring vitality to the worship experience that engages people and makes them want to come back. Use your pastor's valuable time for ministry outreach, education, and worship development, those tasks he or she is specially trained for. Make use of the creativity he or she brings to the table. And even if your pastor is part-time, you can support his or her ministry with perks like extra vacation or sabbatical and study time away to compensate for a more humble salary package.

Be creative about training lay members to assist with pastoral duties such as home visitation and teaching confirmation. Many denominations have provisions for deacons, elders, or lay pastors to serve communion, preach, and carry out administrative duties. Historically, Protestant churches have understood ourselves to be a "priesthood of all believers," and that characterization may become more significant in the future, as lay leaders share more ministry tasks with clergy.

Creative staffing options will shift more of the active ministry to lay leaders, or they may lead your church to do more focused, streamlined programming. The positive is that, with less paid staff time, the ministry offered to the community is made up of whatever spiritual gifts the laity lay on the altar, and a blessed uniqueness may emerge from each congregation's gifts offered to the community.

YOKES, MERGERS, AND OTHER COLLABORATIONS

Formal partnership with another congregation is one way a church can right-size its ministry for greater vitality. Two churches that are yoked have separate buildings, governing boards, and programs, but share a pastor. Federated churches join in common use of a building, programs, and a pastor, but maintain their separate denominational affiliations.

A legal church merger may involve two churches selling property, pooling financial assets, and adopting a new name. In my interviews, I found denominational representatives ambivalent about mergers, especially when one of the two church's buildings continues to be used after the merger. "We tried to put one together . . . and people told me it felt like a takeover," one regional pastor told me. "A merger cannot be authentic if one [church] loses their building and another keeps theirs. There's always resentment, the feeling of being taken over by another church."

One Catholic lay man told me his parish was resisting a merger planned by his diocese because the two churches involved had a troubled, competitive history. A UCC laywoman confided to me her fear that, as her working-class church began merger conversation with a wealthier church across town, her church would get the short end of the stick in negotiations, even though they were the "healthier" congregation.

Mergers often come about when two churches near each other are both declining in size. While it may seem logical to combine and cut expenses, the reality is that even two churches of the same denomination may be entirely different in character. In addition, the hoped-for gains in vitality do not always occur.

David Raymond, a church consultant in the ELCA (Evangelical Lutheran Church in America), identifies three types of mergers: continuation, rebirth, and absorption. In the first, two congregations join together in an effort to boost their chances for survival while doing ministry in roughly the same way they always have. In a rebirth, two churches both dissolve and shed their buildings and staff, starting over together as a new entity. In absorption, a larger, more vital church will "adopt" a declining church, and the members of the latter will be absorbed into the culture of the larger one.

An ELCA study of mergers since 1988 showed that 75 percent of absorption mergers have resulted in numerical growth. Rebirth mergers led to growth for 38 percent of churches studied, and only 18 percent of continuation mergers went on to grow. Additionally, 36 percent of the churches that chose a continuation merger were eventually closed.[5]

While not all mergers result in growth, the impulse of churches to turn to each other for renewed vitality is a good idea in principle. Fewer buildings to maintain and shared staffing equals less expense. Shared programming may result in a bigger pool of participants and livelier engagement as the "critical mass" of a group is increased. In some cases, maintaining two locations with one common mission and shared staff (multisite churches) may increase the reach each church has into the community.

Jim Tomberlin and Warren Bird, in their book *Better Together*, believe that the mergers of an earlier time, which arose out of the desperate need of churches to keep their doors open, may be giving way to a new wave of mergers that are more missional in their outlook. Mergers they studied that involve a stronger *lead church* and a smaller *joining church* may result in:

- Revitalizing the smaller of the two congregations,

- Creating greater ethnic diversity, or

- Broadening the reach of the lead church.[6]

However, these churches merge only after assessing that they can do ministry "better together" than separately, not as a strategy for survival. See Appendix A for an example of a judicatory policy on how to negotiate a merger.

Church of All Nations (CAN) in Columbia Heights, Minnesota, is a unique new church development that found a way to partner with an older congregation. It started when a Korean Presbyterian church began doing outreach to second-generation Koreans. As the outreach grew, they found they were drawing members of other immigrant groups as well. This led to the formation of a new church, Church of All Nations, with a vision of reaching out to an ethnically mixed blend of Christians. When the venture grew too large to continue nesting in the parent church, they sought their own space. Enter Shiloh Bethany Presbyterian Church. The little congregation was mostly Caucasian in membership, and declining in numbers. They were no longer able to maintain their building on their own and had lost a clear sense of their mission. When they were approached by CAN, they thought they might offer their building to the young church in a rental relationship.

5. Raymond, "Blending by Continuation Merger," para. 3 (chart).
6. Tomberlin and Bird, *Better Together*, 11.

But God had something different in mind: a multiethnic merger. After Shiloh Bethany was approached by CAN, one of its members had a dream one night of her church filled with young people she didn't know. She went to church and told the other members about her dream. From there, the merger conversation began. Because CAN was working hard to form its own identity as a new church, the Shiloh Bethany members became the *joining church* and let CAN take the lead in developing that identity in their building. Since their merger in 2006, CAN has continued to grow in diversity, incorporating small, ethnically diverse worshiping groups within its ministry. They also value the older members from Shiloh Bethany who joined them and brought greater age diversity to their membership.

The Springhouse Ministry Center is the result of three congregations in South Minneapolis who are pooling their resources at one ministry location they can all share while maintaining separate congregations. Springhouse was born from the conversation of two frustrated pastors of declining churches in adjacent neighborhoods. One was Salem Lutheran (ELCA) and the other was Lyndale United Church of Christ. Although both struggled financially, they each held valuable property and both had creative, resourceful lay members who were willing to take risks. Over the course of about seven years, a decision was made to pool their resources by selling the UCC building and retrofitting Salem's building for shared use. The Salem congregation also sold a section of their property, which was converted into affordable housing and commercial space.

Just as they were about to begin an extensive 4.2 million dollar remodeling project, a new opportunity presented itself: a third church, First Christian Church (Disciples of Christ), had sold their building to a museum and had been given five years to continue using it while they weighed their options. The Salem and Lyndale churches approached First about whether they also wanted to invest in the partnership. After a short "dating" period, all three churches voted to move ahead together. Pastor Jen Nagel of Salem said, "It took a lot of holy imagination. We didn't know where we were going or what would happen."

Plans were redrawn to incorporate three distinct sanctuary spaces into the remodeled Salem site. Today, the congregations all meet at the same time each Sunday, rotating between worship spaces. They share a Sunday School program and some community mission projects but remain three distinct congregations.[7]

7. Moore, "Three Churches Go Condo," para. 6 and author interview.

BUILDING ISSUES

How to deal with a church building that no longer serves the needs of the congregation and its mission is probably the thorniest problem for declining churches. Even after staff and program cuts are made in a right-sizing effort, the building may continue to place a financial burden on the ministry. In my experience, a building with its maintenance requirements can present itself like a needy church member who drains energy from the entire congregation. Many church leaders spend a disproportionate amount of time in meetings discussing the maintenance of their facilities, while faith formation, mission projects, worship, and prayer are neglected.

On the other hand, church buildings are loaded with emotional weight, since they are imposing symbols of belonging and purpose for their members. Weddings, funerals, the raising of children, and the forging of life-long friendships have all been contained in this symbolic vessel.

Conversations about ways to use your building must be carried out with both sensitivity to the work of grief and rational consideration of your building as a financial asset. It is vitally important to remember that just because the congregation may need to part with its building does not necessarily mean you will have to end your ministry. In some cases, the ministry is revitalized by shedding an inappropriate building; in other cases, the building becomes the site of a new ministry. It is my belief that conversations about the feasibility of owning a certain building should be distinct from conversations about the vitality or viability of a congregation's ministry.

In addition, remember that liquidation of property is a decision that should be made in consultation with the wider church. Churches may be restricted not only by denominational polity, but also by building codes, zoning ordinances, and the community's openness to new uses for your building.[8] In chapter 9, we will address some of the emotional content involved in a decision to sell a church building.

---

8. Congregations that own historic buildings in prominent locations sometimes face opposition from historic preservation groups and local ordinances if they wish to convert property for a new use.

RELOCATION

Many churches find that demographic changes in their neighborhoods make relocation seem like a good way to regain vitality or extend their lifespan. In the twentieth century, many urban churches were born and then died within one or two generations. Before they closed, some first left the inner cities to follow "white flight" migration patterns. (Several of the urban churches I interviewed had relocated a decade or so before they finally closed.) They found the ethnic change their neighborhoods had undergone made it difficult to be relevant to new neighbors, so they moved to where their Euro-American members had moved: the outer rings of the city. In some cases, these moves have contributed to continued growth. In other cases, relocated churches lasted only a few more years after relocation.

Churches thinking about relocation should consider carefully the needs of the neighborhoods they plan to leave behind. While relocation may allow a congregation to survive longer by moving to an area where a more familiar socioeconomic group is clustered, there is a cost borne by the urban dwellers who are left behind. These people still need churches and the "social capital" they provide as gathering places and social service providers.

Congregations and even whole denominations must come to terms with the reality that relocating churches has sometimes left the homeless poor seeking shelter in the doorways of their abandoned buildings. If the church is serious about its call to serve the poor, both rural and urban, we must find ways to finance the existence of ministry sites in places where the membership cannot sustain its own costs.

Urban ministries might be encouraged to sell their valuable property but maintain more cost-efficient ministry sites in the same neighborhoods. Urban and suburban congregations could team up in configurations like those noted by Tomberlin and Bird to share ministry resources between two merged congregations. Multicultural and ecumenical models could be explored in which space for worship and social services could be shared, such as SpringHouse Ministry Center has done.

RENTED OR SHARED SPACE

Since the building may be one of the biggest barriers to viability, some churches have chosen to pursue renting out space to other organizations.

Churches that share space with other nonprofit organizations need to engage in intentional conversation with their partners to avoid misunderstandings. Insurance policies, zoning regulations, and denominational requirements should all be explored before engaging in a shared use agreement. This option may or may not lead to renewed vitality, depending on how the congregation makes use of its opportunities.

When Pastor Lee came to our church to ask if his congregation might share space in our building, I felt that he was sent by God. His young congregation needed space; we had a large upstairs meeting hall that we rarely used. But before we shook hands on a "match made in heaven," I called our insurance company. They helped us draft a shared use contract that included specifics about how and when the space would be shared. The Hmong church purchased an insurance policy from the same company, so that both groups were protected should a claim need to be made. We requested from them a below-market monthly donation to cover our ownership costs. A friendship evolved between our congregations that included shared potlucks and worship services, an adult study on Hmong culture, and even a bicultural wedding that built a bridge between two of our families. While the arrangement did not "save" our church, it gave us a unique outreach in the community for the last five years of our ministry, and assisted a young church to be financially sustainable in affordable space.[9]

STRUCTURE

If your congregation is discerning God's call to right-size or close, the old lines of accountability and committee structures may not work anymore. It is time to focus energy on groups that are working well and accomplishing mission goals. Let the Spirit move you outside of your structure to explore new partnerships between existing groups, allowing some groups to dissolve, or letting creative members form new groups in experimental and temporary ways. A church's governing board may suspend its own bylaws for a specific period of time to try working in a new way; if the experiment works, the new format can be encoded in its constitution.

Don't be tempted to do more or work harder. Instead, let your congregation move toward those things that fulfill your mission, even in small ways, giving the congregation a sense of accomplishment of ministry goals.

9. In an added twist, when the host church was closed, the nesting congregation was allowed by the Presbytery to continue using the building.

Don't worry too much about "breaking the rules" of a former era in your church. Allow for a little more chaos in order to bring new leaders and ideas into the circle.

At Pastor Mark's church, the entire congregation began functioning as the governing board in its final years. Everybody was invited to everything. All members were given voice and vote in decision making. Nonmembers could speak at meetings, but they were not given a vote, and no proxy votes by absent members were allowed.

While a church is required by its denomination and nonprofit law to maintain certain aspects of the organization, such as a governing board, treasurer, and/or trustees, you can still be a church without a worship committee and a Christian education board. Be sure you understand what type of structure is required by your denomination, and then be creative within those limits.

MISSION IMPOSSIBLE?

Many small churches have budgets that have been whittled down over the years, cutting mission and program dollars to preserve basic maintenance and staff costs. Is it possible to engage in mission as a church that is relocating or closing? Yes! The most exciting stories of churches that right-sized or closed are stories of generous legacies passed on.

- Riverview Church sold their building for about $600,000 to another congregation. They spread the money among several mission projects in their former neighborhood, their denomination's fund for new church development, and the two churches their former members migrated to.

- Hartford Church gave its small, rural building to be used by a tutoring center for youth.

- West Valley Church's building was given to a new church development and was then converted by that church into a community clinic.

- Gloria's church continues to maintain a scholarship fund for Chinese American students.

Ironically, renewed generosity may spring from a congregation when they decide to sell their building or even close permanently. There is never a time in the church's life when mission is impossible. In fact, if churches come to feel their mission is "impossible," they have ceased to be churches.

REMOVING OBSTACLES TO VITALITY

Sometimes the barrier to vital ministry is not financial but emotional. Congregations that are willing to address old conflicts and pursue reconciliation may unearth the resources they need to regain vitality.

Pastor Karl left the ministry after a personal crisis involving an extramarital affair. He and his wife engaged in counseling and rebuilt their marriage, but he was obliged to take a break from professional ministry for about two years.

Then his regional pastor, willing to take a chance on him again, told him about a church that was on the path to closure. St. Mark's UCC was a tiny country church that had been yoked with a Methodist church, but the Methodists had decided to withdraw from the yoke. The regional pastor assumed that there were no options for pastoral leadership and that the church would now close its doors.

Karl accepted the call but said in our interview that he "came under false pretenses." He had no intention to close the church if he could avoid it. In his mind "closure was not an option." Nevertheless, he told his regional pastor he would serve the church for one year to assist them with a discernment process.

At his first board meeting, the board told him "we don't want to disband." But Karl made it clear that "things as they are cannot continue." He suggested that they would need to reinvent themselves. It was agreed that they would discuss their future together for one year, then make a decision. "Plan A was to close the church," he said.

Pastor Karl enlisted the help of a conference staff member skilled in conflict facilitation. An assessment process was set up involving individual meetings with every member. He started with fringe members first, moving on to key lay leaders last. Each member was asked to come to the church to meet with the pastor and regional staff member. They were asked if they wanted to keep the church open and to identify the church's core purpose. Then they were asked for specific commitments. Would they attend worship? Help with projects? Give financially? And finally, he asked them to put aside long-standing grudges in order to help the church move forward.

Karl reminded them of his own story, which they had heard at the time of his hiring: he had committed a sin that was revealed to his former congregation. His family and the wider church had given him another chance. St. Mark's had hired him, giving him another chance. He experienced grace and forgiveness. "When I came, it was a feeling of acceptance, tolerance, forgiveness," he said.

"So, when someone said, 'I really don't like that person. I don't want to forgive them,' I said, 'I'm kind of an unforgiveable person, too. I have this history that's less than sterling, but I feel all kinds of forgiveness in this church. Why can't you share that with some others?'"

In this way, Karl appealed to the congregation to put aside their differences for the sake of their church's future. After a year of discernment, the congregation decided to continue its ministry with the part-time ministry of Pastor Karl. At the time of our interview, he had been serving them for twelve fruitful years.

BETHEL UCC, CAHOKIA

At Bethel UCC in Cahokia, Illinois, Rev. Carol Shanks's congregation saw the writing on the wall: they had less than three years' worth of cash reserves to continue as they were. They needed an experienced pastor to help them decide what they should do next, and Shanks was called in. She listened one on one with members and engaged in group conversation about their options. They also studied the needs of their surrounding community. Then the congregation "dated" three community organizations to dialog about a shared relationship. One was Hoyleton Ministries, a nonprofit organization serving at-risk youth. Recognizing that they had a long-standing mission partnership with Hoyleton, and observing the agency's enthusiasm about using the building, the Bethel congregation decided to generously give their building to Hoyleton and proceed with closure.

But just as the plan began to unfold, Hoyleton approached the church and suggested a shared use arrangement in which both organizations could serve the community under one roof. The Bethel members gratefully accepted the invitation to continue worshiping in shared space but fully expected that their closure would be complete in the next couple years.

That was not what God planned, however. Two years after the shared arrangement was put into place, Bethel was still meeting for worship and mission. Inspired to clarify their mission, they decided to engage in the UCC's Open and Affirming dialog process to discern whether they would be publicly welcoming of gay and lesbian Christians. Rev. Shanks calls it "one of the most spiritual experiences of my life." Over time, the membership of Bethel has changed, as some members passed away, and new members came. Today, they involve about twenty five people in worship, a number that has stayed consistent for over a decade.[10]

RELINQUISHING

As you read the various options to closure presented above, you may be inspired to experiment with new options for your church. Or you may be thinking, "We've explored all those options. They all led to dead ends." If your congregation feels that there is little chance of sustaining a vital ministry in the future, you should make a plan for relinquishing the ministry to God's care and completing your ministry together. Revisit the assessment questions in chapter 5 and consider whether it is time to move toward closure before you lose all your spiritual and material resources. In chapter 8 you will hear two stories of churches that made the decision to relinquish their ministry to God and move forward in new ways.

HOW LONG WILL WE LIVE?

Gloria's Chinese congregation has concluded that their congregation will continue to meet together as long as Gloria, who is 94 years old, is able to meet with them. Their scholarship fund for Chinese American students will continue after their closure. Their ministry is primarily to their own circle of members, but they have the means to continue meeting in another church's fellowship room on a monthly basis for their own spiritual nurture, and at their advanced age, this is probably the best option for them.

By contrast, in the church I served, the option of keeping the church open for another year or so, using the bequest of a beloved saint of the church, was discussed and finally rejected. They preferred that the legacy they inherited be used for vital ministry, not "life support."

Whether a church stays open another year or another twenty-five years, longevity is not the goal. No church lasts forever, and longevity is not the marker of our success. The goal should be pursuing the most faithful, vital way of building up the Body of Christ through the growing and gathering of his disciples.

10. Shanks has written a book, *Choosing To Be a What If Church,* about her experience at Bethel.

This chapter has offered stories of creative ways churches maintained or regained vitality and viability through new ways of doing ministry. You may wonder: what if we go through all these changes and our church still closes in a few years? Speaking as a pastor who served a dying congregation for eleven years, I believe the knowledge that your church life together is limited can be a blessing instead of a curse. All life is limited. No local church lasts forever. Only Christ's universal church is eternal. Instead of wondering how long your church will survive, you can change the question to: *how well can we live for the time we have been given by God?*

Members must face this question together. In some cases, breaking up the congregation now will increase spiritual vitality as individual members join new churches where they can live out their faith with more energy. In other cases, closure of a church would mean loneliness and the end of a needed ministry for members who are no longer able to find new spiritual homes.

In true discernment, we don't know what the outcome of our exploration will be. As you consider all the possibilities for your church, don't rush to rule any one of them out too quickly. Take the time to imagine each pathway and ask, with others, "Which path is Christ leading us to explore?"

REFLECTION

All the Israelites grumbled against Moses and Aaron, and the whole assembly said to them, "If only we had died in Egypt! Or in this wilderness! Why is the Lord bringing us to this land only to let us fall by the sword? Our wives and children will be taken as plunder. Wouldn't it be better for us to go back to Egypt?" And they said to each other, "We should choose a leader and go back to Egypt."

Then Moses and Aaron fell face down in front of the whole Israelite assembly gathered there . . . and said to the entire Israelite assembly, "The land we passed through and explored is exceedingly good. If the Lord is pleased with us, he will lead us into that land, a land flowing with milk and honey, and will give it to us. Only do not rebel against the Lord."

NUMBERS 14:2–5, 6–9A

- When faced with possible choices, does your congregation express the impulse to stay as they are or to regress back to an earlier time? How and when do they express trust and confidence in the future, even when times are tough?

- In a group, discuss some of the paths outlined in this chapter and those paths your congregation has already pursued. Have each person independently spend reflection time imagining each path and where it might lead. Then gather and discuss what you imagined. How do members of the group feel as each path is explored? Which paths seem to move forward? Which move backward?

8

A Tale of Two Closures

Following the current trend of decline is not ministry. Nostalgia is not ministry. Enjoying one another's company at potlucks is not ministry.

Pastor Mark

MANY PEOPLE SIMPLY DON'T want to face the reality that churches are closing their doors. If they do bring up closure, the topic usually arises under a cloud of threat, such as when someone says, "If we don't get more members, one of these days our church will close!"

A young Catholic man said to me, "Oh, I think it's awful when they close churches! Those poor people who put all their money into it, they deserve to be married and buried there!" A pastor confessed to me that, when he was first called to a church considering closure, his attitude was, "I'm not going to let them close. I don't believe in that." A regional pastor I interviewed said, "I have never seen a church closure go well." And another said, "I don't know why you want to interview me. I'm focusing on keeping churches *open*."

All these responses have led me to think that the first key to accomplishing a healthy closure of a church is accepting that such a thing sometimes must happen. Church closure isn't just the result of a "disease" contracted by a few unlucky congregations. It is not necessarily a sign of lagging faith, internal conflict, or hard-hearted denominational bodies. As long as we hold these assumptions, church closure will always be a taboo subject, and the closures will be painful.

Many times churches die for the same reason people die: they have reached the end of their lifespans. In some cases, staying open is draining the spiritual energy and financial resources of a congregation, as they lose their capacity for self-determination. A closure may actually increase the spiritual energy of the members.

Is it possible that God is calling your church to close its doors? This chapter explores ways that a congregation can end its ministry in healthy gratitude for God's work done in that place, and make a plan for a future that includes doing ministry in new ways. You will read about two very different churches that relinquished their ministry to God in faithful ways.

WHAT MAKES A CLOSURE HEALTHY?

What does it mean for a closure to be "healthy"? In my research and interviews, I looked for congregations that experienced closure with these characteristics:

- They were able to move or end their ministry without heightened emotional conflict.

- The spiritual energy of members was not drained by the process.

- They were able to manage the stewardship of their assets in ways that preserved those assets for uses that were consistent with their historical mission, and/or emerging needs in their communities.

- They were able to maintain right relationship with the wider church.

- They understood their local churches to be part of Christ's universal church.

- They engaged in expressions of corporate grief and found theological anchors for their actions.

- While their church doors closed, the members stayed open to ways they could redirect their energy toward new mission and ministry in the future.

Mt. Tabor and Riverview were two very different churches, but each of their stories traces a faithful line of prayerful discernment. Pay attention to the way the leaders of these two churches navigated the path of discernment with their members, as well as the persistence of members in exploring every option.

MT. TABOR METHODIST

Mt. Tabor Methodist Church found itself pressed to make not one decision but three in the span of a few years: (1) whether to sell their parsonage, (2) whether to repair or demolish their church building, and (3) whether to stay together as a congregation. Each of these decisions stood alone, but they all impacted each other.

Mt. Tabor had served its small North Dakota community for nearly a century when discussions about closure began. At that time, they were yoked with two other churches and Pastor Mark had served them for over a decade.

Mark cited a number of reasons why the church experienced decline: the community was losing population ("Even the nursing home is losing residents," Mark said). An unpopular previous pastor had driven some members away. And the congregation had resisted change over the years. There was no effort made toward new leadership development. "Some leaders have been in place for decades," Mark said.

The church had dreamed of doing outreach into the Hispanic community, but Mark felt the congregation no longer had the ability to take on a new venture. With loss of critical mass came the loss of energy for programming. On the positive side, the church distributed Christmas baskets in the community and was generous in financial gifts to denominational mission and apportionments. Some of its benevolent giving came from bequested gifts.

After a decade as their pastor, Mark and his congregation began a conversation about possible closure. It began when the governing board was discussing the church's ninetieth anniversary. Someone said, "We better celebrate now; we might not be here in ten years for our hundredth." This comment inspired the congregation to plan a ninetieth birthday celebration that would honor their history. The church was cleaned thoroughly and pieces of the church's china set were sold as souvenirs. Many people were invited to the event and a lot of work was put in. In fact, Mark says it was the last time the congregation was motivated to do a big project together.

That same year, Pastor Mark assembled data on the church's membership and finances. The figures showed that membership and worship attendance had dropped 57 percent in the past decade, while expenses rose 46 percent. An income subsidy from the conference was paid to the church each year. And by the time of the ninetieth anniversary, funds were being withdrawn from reserves for meeting operating expenses.

Mark admitted this research helped him understand why things felt the way they did at Mt. Tabor. When I asked how church leaders took the information, he said, "They couldn't deny it." But he added that, for awhile, the general response was, "Yes, we're getting smaller, but look, we're still giving as much as we used to!" As you recall from chapter 3, denial is common in the first stages of assessing a church's vitality and viability.

After the anniversary, the congregation's energy waned. Pastor Mark began calling the governing board together regularly for focused conversation about their options. That spring, the district superintendent (DS), Harvey, was invited to a meeting of the governing board. Pastor Mark invited those present to recall the highlights of their ninety-one years of history. Harvey assured them that the conference "does not close churches." In his district, this is initiated by the congregation and approved by the conference. Harvey helped them put their church's situation in historical perspective: "The conference has seen more churches close than are in existence today," he said. He told them about various churches he had worked with that had invested their legacies in alternate mission projects, such as maintenance of a historic cemetery, a church camp, or a favorite charitable organization. The DS was suggesting that the congregation had wide latitude to use the proceeds of their building and assets as they saw fit.[1]

Harvey suggested that a perpetual fund could be established to care for the church's cemetery, and a local cemetery board could be set up to manage it. The parsonage could be given to another congregation or sold, with the proceeds directed to a purpose of the congregation's choice. He said he believed it was healthier for the congregation to make this decision than the conference.

As to the question of what would happen to the members, they would be given freedom to choose new churches or be placed on the rolls of the closest United Methodist church, according to United Methodist policy.

A secretary recorded these poignant notes from the meeting that evening:

> It's hard to talk about it. It's hard to make decisions. . . . There is no right or wrong way in how to disband. [Harvey] made a philosophical statement: as people grow old, why not make decisions while you are still able, while you are strong enough, there's more

1. This is not the policy of all United Methodist conferences. For example, in Wisconsin, the assets of churches that close are funneled into new church development projects or are transferred to another church in the case of a merger.

hope and opportunity. How many people will die in the next five years, and then you get to the point where you have to close."

The following year, five members of the church died. No new members were welcomed or baptized.

In a letter sent to the congregation that spring, Mark laid out several options the congregation might consider, including renting space from another organization, federating with another church, merging with another church, or complete closure and disbursement of members. He cited the examples Harvey had mentioned and noted ways that churches disperse their funds and property. He assured the congregation that they would have "much latitude" in making property and continuation plans; the conference was not going to force a decision. However, he quoted Harvey, who had encouraged them to "act while we have strength and not put off hard decisions."

"When the inevitable occurs," Mark wrote, "[a church's] options are much more limited and may even be decided by someone else. This is not a future any one of us wishes to have." As subsequent meetings took place, minutes from the meetings were sent to all the members, including the names of who said what. This helped keep the process as transparent as possible.

In June, another letter outlining options to consider was sent to the congregation by Pastor Mark, and a meeting with a potluck supper was held to discuss which ones might be pursued further. Each option included suggestions on how the sanctuary and parsonage would be used or disposed of. One option was to sell the parsonage and use the proceeds of the sale to demolish the church building, which was now in a state of dangerous ill repair.

At the June meeting, the congregation voted by a two-to-one margin to recommend discontinuing the ministry in one year's time. To abide by United Methodist process, a special charge conference was scheduled with the district superintendent to take the vote again in August. In anticipation of the congregation's grief being unleashed, Pastor Mark wrote in another letter, "We do need to find positive ways to express those feelings in ways that help rather than hurt ourselves and the people around us." He spoke of moving forward with "the same spirit of love, cooperation, and compassion which have been hallmarks of this church . . . needed now more than ever." The letter went so far as to explain how people could transfer or retain membership and the choices facing them in the closure process down the road.

However, this letter turned out to be premature, because when the August meeting occurred, the process of closure was halted. The district superintendent seemed to back away from the congregation's readiness to close. He pointed out that the church could continue to function with a very small administrative board, for example. "Five members are all it takes to be a Methodist church," he said. Notes from this meeting read: "[Harvey] indicated the conference is in no rush to make us close, that's up to the church, not D.S." One member said she felt rushed to close, and "It would not be possible to dispose of the property [in one year]." Another suggested they hire someone to do building maintenance to relieve the burden on volunteers. Two members said they wanted to stay open. At the same time, one lay leader, Joe, admitted he was tired of church leadership. He had served for sixteen years and was "stretched too thin." "The load that [Joe] carries is what started this discussion. Nominating committee has been reassigning the same people to the same offices for the past years." The congregation was dividing.

One possible explanation for the district superintendent's reticence to pursue closure was that the church was providing a third of Pastor Mark's salary and there was no plan in place to provide him with another call. Another reality was that Mt. Tabor was still healthy enough financially to pay its apportionments and give to various mission organizations.

A "straw vote" was taken: ten members now voted to "remain Mt. Tabor UMC," four voted to continue as a Methodist church but move to another location, and seven voted to transfer all memberships to another church. The majority was not ready to pursue closure, and nearly half wanted to continue worshiping together in their building. However, one new development occurred that night: the group decided to pursue sale of the parsonage. This effort proceeded in the coming year.

Nearly a year later, Mark again sent out a congregational letter expressing his feelings of affection for the congregation he had been with for nearly fourteen years. Their membership was now thirty-nine souls, with worship attendance averaging seventeen. Mark wrote,

> The main purpose of any church is to be in ministry as a fellowship of believers in Christ," he wrote. If our only reasons to continue being an organized church are to worship in our own building and to care for just our own few members, then, in my opinion, we would not be fulfilling God's calling. Following the current trend of decline is not ministry. Nostalgia is not ministry. Enjoying one another's company at potlucks is not ministry. While our familiar

building and treasured past hold many precious memories, in my
opinion, those reasons alone are not justifications for our continued existence.

In this letter, Mark assumed the task of a prophetic leader. He put
aside his concerns about his own salary and focused on the deeper task
of the church. "Could we be a church fellowship without our building? Is
there a new ministry we should pursue, or should we dissolve our formal
fellowship?" he asked.

Mark again put forth the idea of using the proceeds of the parsonage
sale to fund the demolition of the church building.

> This removal of the church building may be upsetting to you. It
> is hard for me to think about, too, and it is not something I look
> forward to. . . . If we were to let go of the building and continue as
> a church, it would remove the burden of maintaining and repair-
> ing. . . . Is it good stewardship to sink money into repairs for a
> building that might not be in use for much longer?

He expressed concern for elderly members who would be left with the
burden of selling the church later down the road when energy was more
limited, and spoke of continued ministry that could be done without a
building, including their scholarship program and other mission projects.

> Even in death, our church could leave a lasting legacy of blessing
> for others. . . . My intention is not to alarm or frighten you. I love
> you more than any building, and I would be negligent not to help
> you address the realities facing us.

Finally, Mark invited everyone to a potluck to talk more.

Despite the reluctance of both an aging congregation and a timid judicatory, Pastor Mark was haunted by a sense of responsibility that looked
beyond his own salary and the comfort of his members. His own communication suggested that he was leaning toward the idea of using the proceeds of the sale of the parsonage to demolish the church building. He was
aware that the conference would not have funds for demolition, and the
building would probably languish in decay if the congregation didn't attend
to it. "It's our church, we're the ones responsible for it," he told me. "It's our
responsibility to take it down."

That spring, the congregation voted to sell the parsonage to an inter-
ested buyer who would also buy the adjacent church lot. However, the sale
was contingent on the sanctuary building being razed. One participant at

the meeting asked, "Does a yes vote mean we are voting to tear down the church?" In an emotional moment, Pastor Mark answered, "Yes, that's what it means." The motion passed fourteen to one.

The minutes of this meeting show an immediate and marked change of mood once the parsonage sale was settled. Making one decision had opened the door to make others. It was suggested that $35,000 in proceeds from the sale of the parsonage be used to demolish the dilapidated church building. The group went on to discuss possible uses for the remainder, including a cemetery fund, and (in a bizarre twist) repairs to the church building so it could be used for a few more months. The conversation included discussion of what would be done with furnishings, sacred objects, and historical documents. Clearly, the group was now emotionally ready to move forward with closure. However, Harvey urged them not to officially close until all the property was legally disposed of.

Now three years into its discernment process, the group proceeded with a $16,000 repair to the church's chimney so they could continue to use the building for another year. It was said, "We're still here. We're not ready to move. This is North Dakota. We need heat."

Although the record shows the congregation had voted to raze the building, they stayed open to proposals from a buyer who would move it off the property. At one point, the group even voted on a proposal to allow a new church development to lease the building in place. In the long run, Pastor Mark said selling the parsonage took "four times longer than expected" because of uncertainty about what would happen to the adjacent sanctuary.

The congregation still faced a decision about whether to continue together as a congregation. In an effort to make this decision, a conference staff member was called upon to do an assessment and "visioning meeting." She assessed all three congregations in the yoke by presenting them with the following questions:

1. Do we invite people?

2. Do we make disciples?

3. Do we worship regularly?

4. Do we nurture spiritual growth?

5. Do we pray for the world and one another?

6. Do we participate in local and global mission?

7. Do we meet our financial obligations?

8. Do we share in mission and pay apportionment?

On this slim evidence, the conference staff person announced that, based on her assessment, the church should remain open and add a Hispanic ministry outreach program to its ministry. Pastor Mark responded to this development with "mixed feelings," to say the least. At this point, he had already given considerable energy to preparing his congregation for the work of grief and closure.

On reflection about the conference staff's assessment, Mark said: "Her job is to help churches grow. . . . I could see her point. On paper we look viable. We are paying our apportionment. We have savings. We are praying for each other. We have regular worship. But a couple areas are not as good as we could be." The conference visitor and her response "added to our conflicted feeling." He proceeded to follow his heart despite the judicatory recommendation to stay open.

At the end of the third year of discernment, the congregation finally voted on ending the congregation's ministry. The procedure for making such a decision was "fuzzy," Mark said, because the Book of Discipline, while being clear on how to sell property, had no clear guidelines on how to dissolve a congregation.

Unlike some United Methodist churches, the Dakota Conference allows rural churches to make their own decisions about how to disperse their assets, and this was the next challenge. Some funds were set aside in the hopes that a Hispanic ministry project could be started in the community. A cemetery fund was established, and various mission projects received funds.

In our interviews, Pastor Mark was philosophical about the process he had walked his church through.

> Churches are human institutions in part, not entirely. The spirit of God works through them, too. But the human part is limited. It's finite. Mortal. So, theologically, it will not last forever, and in a rural setting with all the changes over the last fifty years in rural America, the odds are stacked against particular churches. Not every rural church is going to close, but the weakest will. And yet—why do we die? To make room for somebody else. I can see, for some of these people, if you let this institution go, [if you] go through the hard work of grieving, disposing of property, you are freed to do other things. And I can see beyond the death to new life. I need to help them see what eternal life is.

He compared the "eternal life of the soul" with what eternal life might look like for an institution: "Eternal life is an unproven reality. With churches, it's more concrete. You can see what happens afterward, in real time. You can see ministries that might continue. You can see members that move on and do other things."

In the final chapter of Pastor Mark's ministry at Mt. Tabor, the district superintendent offered him a move to a larger, more progressive church in an urban area. He would be required to move before his tiny church had completed its ministry, and he would also have to leave two other congregations he enjoys serving. His spouse, also a pastor, would need to be uprooted from her church as well. This offer was made on the very day when the final vote was taken by the congregation to close. After a feverish couple of days of weighing his options, Pastor Mark decided to stay and see his dying church through to its completion. He still felt a deep loyalty to the church and refused to abandon it for professional advancement.

Because the demolition of the building would prove to be more costly than moving it to another location, a buyer was sought to move it, but no buyer was found. The congregation finally decided to use the proceeds of the parsonage sale to raze the sanctuary. The demolition occurred one autumn weekend, and the debris was buried on farm land owned by a former member. The members of Mt. Tabor all moved on to other churches. Pastor Mark now serves his two remaining churches, each at half time.

Why do I characterize this closure as being successful? The entire process took about four years, with repeated zig-zagging and flip-flopping on the part of the congregation and wider church leaders. A few able-bodied members left the system during the process. But every action along the way was intentional and transparent. Members were given ample opportunities to voice their ideas, concerns, and emotions. Conversations were recorded and shared. Regional leaders were invited into the process but did not dominate or control the outcome. Loyalty to the denomination and church's historic mission were maintained. Pastoral care of members was consistent, and new church homes were found for everyone. Stewardship of property was honored. A vision of future ministry with the Hispanic community was accommodated with a fund. Grief was expressed. And the pastor maintained his professional integrity and his compassionate love for his congregation through every step of the process.

An outsider might see some clumsy maneuvers and mistakes made throughout the process. But a church is a human community, not a machine.

In the same way our family funerals and stages of grief are fraught with strange behavior, a congregation's behavior will not always be orderly and rational. It is faithfulness to God and community that must be maintained.

RIVERVIEW PRESBYTERIAN CHURCH

In contrast to Mt. Tabor's zig-zag process of discernment and closure, Riverview Presbyterian Church took a more direct approach to its process of closing. Riverview was an urban church that had moved twice in its history. When Pastor Bob arrived as their interim pastor, they were located in a neighborhood of starter homes near two large churches, one Catholic and one Lutheran, both of which had their own parochial schools. Mobility in the area was high. Both parochial schools offered reduced tuition for parishioners. These were some of the reasons Bob cited that Riverview could not seem to maintain its critical mass of members.

Pastor Bob was trained as an interim pastor and had specialized in transitional ministry for his entire career before he came to Riverview. "Not long after I got there, the leaders of the church and myself went to the presbytery and told them possible closure was the primary question of this interim time. The presbytery expressed they were aware this church had been struggling and they started instantly getting resources for us." One resource was the book *Ending with Hope*. Another resource Bob found extremely helpful was his connection to two area clergy as a support network. "They had a good working relationship with each other and the wider church, and this made it easier to talk to them about our needs." These two pastors offered resources and pastoral care. They also benefited significantly from Riverview's ultimate decision to disperse its assets in their direction.

Bob's predecessor had been with the church for nearly a decade. During her tenure, she had led them in a lengthy process of discernment and experimentation with church growth strategies, including assertive outreach to new residents and hosting community groups in the building. The church had engaged in a demographic study to track where people were traveling from to church, and they had already discussed a number of alternatives to closure, such as selling the building and worshiping elsewhere. "They just didn't see revitalization from any of it," Bob said. He felt the previous pastor had effectively laid the groundwork for discussion of possible closure and her departure had made them more ready.

When he arrived, there were ninety-four members, and almost everyone stayed active in the church until it closed. About forty-five souls attended worship and the church was still financially solvent. They still offered some programming, including a Wednesday night children's program with dinner that attracted three or four children, and an adult class on Sunday mornings. "They were doing all they could," Bob said. They knew they had enough money in reserves to keep doing ministry as they were for another four to five years, but they weren't convinced this was the right course of action.

Bob's first response was to tell them he would need to have it demonstrated to him that closure was the right way to go. He began by testing the congregation's feelings about the future. "I was trying to find out if this was just five people who had come to me and said that we might close or if there was really a general feeling in the church." He talked one on one with people and researched the status of the congregation. "I kept saying 'Convince me.' I kept waiting for people to come forward and say, 'Listen to our new interim. He thinks we can make it.' And I never heard that."

In retrospect, Bob says his attitude of needing to prove closure was the right course was a helpful one. "If I had agreed with the first consensus, any voice of dissent would have felt marginalized." His skepticism "encouraged open-minded conversation and dissent. It was a helpful approach."

Individually, people told him the same story he was hearing in leadership groups: "We've tried years of revitalization and we have these two large churches with schools anchoring our neighborhood. We know other churches in our neighborhood are struggling." The group message and individual messages were consistent with each other. There were a few voices saying, "I hope we don't have to do this [close the church]." But none saying they shouldn't at least examine it.

A turning point occurred when Pastor Bob wrote his annual report to the congregation. "I wrote, 'Here's what the data shows, what you've said to me and I've tried to do. What do you see? Is it possible God is asking us to be the church in a new way? I'm not the one to make the decision, but all of us together must make it with God's help.'"

A discernment process was begun using *Ending with Hope* as a guideline. Small groups were formed, followed by larger group discussion. There were "talk back sessions" where Bob played back what he was hearing from the small groups to test if he was getting it right. Any issues or concerns were dealt with there. An overnight retreat was planned and thirty-five people attended. It was a time to get away together and thank each other for their mutual ministry.

The discernment process also included discussion about *ecclesiology*—the character of a vital, authentic church. After an adult group explored this topic, the feeling was that Riverview could no longer perform the functions of authentic ministry.

Throughout the discernment phase, emotions were expressed, practical questions were asked, and the group tried "to listen for what God was saying to us and not just what we wanted." At one point, the few younger members spoke from their hearts to the older members: "We're here if we can help you through this process of closing, but if not, we're moving on, because it's not fair for our children to be the only ones in Sunday School. It's not fair for us to feel like our resources aren't building up the church but are merely maintaining something from the past."

"It was the honesty of the young people when they said this out loud. It helped to bring some people along who had been on the fence, as they realized they were going to be twenty people all over age seventy-five. They probably would not have an organist. As it all started to set in, it didn't sound like church anymore to them," Bob said.

Pastor Bob recognized that different people were experiencing grief on different timelines and encouraged the congregation to accommodate each other's need to grieve. "Even the younger people who were more ready were able to wait and be patient and understanding toward those who were reluctant, grieving more. There was no anger or blow-ups or people turning on each other. There was widespread acceptance."

Bob pointed out that his interim training helped with the process, because interims typically don't deal with building and program issues but with "more systemic/family systems issues around the emotional nature of the congregation." He engaged in a lot of "hallway ministry," informal conversation after worship, keeping himself accessible.

At the time the church voted on closure, they knew they had help from the neighbor churches. They knew the presbytery was supportive and involved, and they had completed their own discernment. They had not yet pursued sale of the building and didn't know whether the presbytery would allow them to control the disbursement of their assets. There was no research yet on the value of their building. Nevertheless, 90 percent voted to "blend" their membership in with two other churches as new spiritual homes. No formal merger arrangement with these churches was made.

Once the vote to disband the congregation and sell the building had been taken, the congregation immediately formed four committees and was "very organized" about implementing their decision. The four committees were:

- Inventory/cleaning committee

- History committee

- Closing ceremony committee

- Liaison committee

The inventory group took change of dispersing every object "not nailed down," including sacred objects, and they cleaned the building. The historical committee made contact with donors of significant objects to see what the donors' wishes were. They also wrote and published a history of the church. The closing ceremony group planned the congregation's final weekend and produced a different book for that occasion. The liaison committee matched members with new churches. Bob assisted this group with their task, profiling each member's gifts and interests and creating a spiritual inventory to share with their new pastors.

As the closure plans progressed, the congregation pursued the sale of their building through a real estate agent, and it was sold for over $600,000 to an African American congregation. He says the Riverview members were "very relieved" they were able to sell to another church.

Because Presbyterian congregations are connectional, the presbytery generally controls how assets are to be used after a closure. In this case, the presbytery worked with the members on asset distribution. "They saw we were trying to be faithful in the process and they wanted to reward that" [by giving the members some control over the sale]. "We could have dumped the building on the presbytery," Bob pointed out.

In addition to over $600,000 in building assets, the church held about $150,000 in various endowment accounts. Some of this was dispersed to local mission projects, including a neighborhood service organization for the elderly that the church had supported. The presbytery received a gift of $200,000 to be used for church redevelopment or new church starts.

The remaining funds were dispersed through the members who affiliated with new churches. Each member took $7,000 with them to their new church. This, along with the $200,000 gift to the presbytery and $40,000 to local mission organizations, created a huge windfall for faith and service groups. After doing his own calculations, Pastor Bob reported to the congregation that the mission dollars they dispersed due to the closure equaled the total mission giving they had accomplished *in the previous 14 years.* This perspective helped some people see the closure in a positive light. "The members were able to feel like they made an instant impact on their new churches," Bob said.

On the last weekend, two worship services were scheduled. The first was just for the members, who shared an intimate service, "being honest about our grief, with space to talk and share about our history and closure," Bob remembered. The second service was "for the whole world." Nearly 450 people attended, including members of the presbytery, the two welcoming churches, and "anybody we had done mission with."

In the process of resettlement, the congregation split into two groups. Of the ninety members present when the church closed, only five refused to reaffiliate. The rest joined one of the two welcoming congregations. The welcoming churches were prepared to bring in the new members. Bob gave an inventory of members' spiritual gifts to the pastors. A church directory was produced in which every member was listed with their new church affiliation. Today, former members still gather for occasional reunions and funerals.

Pastor Bob mused during our interview: "They had tried revitalization stuff for a decade. They needed a fresh start and that was where the resurrection piece came in. Even though it wasn't the best of all possible worlds, it was better than the other options.

"Every piece fell into place as well as it could. We helped each other to be honest with each other. They knew they had a quality ministry that wasn't attracting people. They had judicatory support. They had options to consider."

Pastor Bob said his own ideas about church closure changed in this experience. "Churches are born, grow, get sick, fight, and die. We have this idea of churches having a perpetual existence when that's probably unrealistic for any congregation. We want to be faithful as long as we're vibrant and vibrant as long as we're faithful. It doesn't have to be seen as such a failure."

"I felt like I was involved in the discernment as well. . . . It was important to enter with the way my heart was leading me at the time. . . . They were a gifted, hopeful group. Through their consistent message to me and their strength in facing up to that message, I went, 'Maybe this is what God is saying.'" The congregation found a healthy way to deal with their loss when they were able to say, "Maybe we're not closing, maybe we're being church in a new way."

IS THERE A RIGHT WAY TO CLOSE?

The Mt. Tabor and Riverview churches each had a unique way of dealing with discernment and closure. One was urban and one rural. One was in a community that had the capacity for a new church to use its building; the other did not. One was staffed by a faithful, long-term pastor, the other by a transitional pastor who only stayed two years. One congregation moved in a relatively straight line from discernment to closure. The other church zig-zagged between multiple options, making one difficult decision at a time. These stories illustrate the fact that there is no one "right" way to accomplish a healthy closure. But some common attributes of these churches should be noted.

HEALTHY CHURCHES HAVE HEALTHY LEADERS

The most obvious gift I observed in closing churches was access to good leaders, both lay and clergy. These include:

- Experienced clergy who engender trust among the congregation
- Pastors with experience in transitional or interim ministry
- Lay members who are trusted as spiritual leaders in the congregation
- Lay members who have experience with migration, such as moving to a new place or changing churches in the past
- Memories and stories of a church's history that inspire gratitude
- Lay, clergy, and wider church leaders with the capacity to be transparent, patient, and sensitive to others' feelings in an atmosphere of collaboration

HEALTHY CHURCHES USE TRANSITIONAL EVENTS AS OPPORTUNITIES

A church that is self-aware will use any new opportunity to evaluate whether change is needed. The most obvious time to assess a church's state of health is during a pastoral transition. This is an opportunity to connect with God for fresh direction in your mission, and to connect with a wider church representative about options for pastoral leadership.

Other transitional events, such as a major building repair or an anniversary, are great opportunities to ask, "How is God connecting our past to our future and what are our priorities at this time?" Rapid demographic changes may be another occasion for serious conversation about the church's changing mission field. You may ask: "What is God doing in our neighborhood, and how can we help?"

HEALTHY CHURCHES ARE NOT AFRAID TO TALK

In every healthy closure I studied, there were members and pastoral leaders who were willing to have *multiple conversations over extended periods of time* about options for change, closure, or movement of the church's ministry setting. Remember from chapter 3 that denial and avoidance are common among many members. There must be members of a church family who are willing to speak up and offer new ideas and feelings in formal and informal settings. Likewise, leaders must watch for "teachable moments," tipping points and times when the Holy Spirit intervenes to help the group speak the truth to one another in love, whether part of a scheduled discernment process or not. We may not always feel we are in control of what happens next, but in the church, we can trust that God *is*.

HEALTHY CHURCHES EXPERIMENT WITH CREATIVE OPTIONS

One interviewee told me of a member of her church who said, "If we can't do ministry in this building, I don't want to do it anymore." This attitude is a good way to murder a church. Instead, congregations should be encouraged to try new behaviors to see what feels right and what doesn't, before rushing to a decision about a new direction. Try worshipping together in another location one Sunday. Form partnership projects with other area churches, such as a joint choir, Bible study, or shared mission project that can lead to further dialog about shared ministry. Try "dating" other nonprofit organizations, as was done by Bethel Church in chapter 7.

HEALTHY CHURCHES SEEK WIDER CHURCH SUPPORT

The healthiest churches I interviewed had a history of relating well to their wider church bodies, and the wider church had an intentional process of assisting churches with transition options. In some regions of the country, church closures have become common, and resources have been developed to assist them. However, some denominations are currently channeling many of their resources toward revitalization and new church development, and they may not yet be tuned to the needs of declining churches. Simply asking your regional pastor about assistance with discernment about closure may help him or her understand your needs and be more responsive.

HEALTHY CHURCHES UNDERSTAND WHAT THE CHURCH IS FOR

"Nostalgia is not ministry," Pastor Mark wrote to his dying congregation. He understood that the church's ministry is meant to be an expression of Christ's Word and work. While churches in most of recorded history have clung to property, institutional structures, and local liturgical traditions, these things are not necessarily required in order to carry out the ministry Christ calls us to.

So what *is* the church for? It is for us what it was for Christ, as he said in Luke 4:18–19: "*The Spirit of the Lord is on me, because he has anointed me to proclaim good news to the poor. He has sent me to proclaim freedom for the prisoners and recovery of sight for the blind, to set the oppressed free, to proclaim the year of the Lord's favor.*"

It is the work entrusted to us in Christ's Great Commission, in Matthew 29:19-20: "*Go and make disciples of all nations, baptizing them in the name of the Father and of the Son and of the Holy Spirit, and teaching them to obey everything I have commanded you.*" Regardless of the institutional strength of a local church, a healthy congregation focuses its attention on continuing this calling to share the Good News.

This Good News is also for us. Despite decline in church participation, some congregations have weathered major transitions, relocations, even complete dissolution, with hope and faith in God's future for continued ministry in new forms. There is always grief and loss, but Christians can move forward in the confidence we receive from the cross of Christ: God is bigger than all deaths and endings, and God does not abandon us.

REFLECTION

Very truly, I tell you, unless a grain of wheat falls into the earth and dies, it remains just a single grain; but if it dies, it bears much fruit.

JOHN 12:24 (NRSV)

- Review the story of your own church's discernment process. What have you learned together so far? What future steps need to be taken?

- As you review the list of attributes of churches that accomplished healthy closures, ask yourself which of these attributes your church has that it can use at this time. How can your congregation maintain or even strengthen its spiritual energy at this time, so that you are not depleted by your ministry tasks?

- What kind of fruit might be borne if you relinquished your current form of ministry to God? What does God want for your future, individually or together?

9

Laying the Foundation
for Future Ministry

We took such a violent battering from the storm that the next day
they began to throw the cargo overboard. On the third day, they threw
the ship's tackle overboard with their own hands. When neither sun
nor stars appeared for many days and the storm continued raging, we
finally gave up all hope of being saved.

ACTS 27:18–20 (NRSV)

IN THE BOOK OF Acts, chapter 27, there is a wonderful adventure story
about Paul's experience with a shipwreck. Paul was a prisoner at the time
and was transported by ship across the Mediterranean, bound for a Roman prison. He was accompanied by a group of fellow prisoners, a Roman
army officer named Julius, the soldiers who guarded the prisoners, and the
sailors who manned the ship. The ship was headed into a stormy season,
and Paul warned the crew of the danger, but they decided to forge ahead.

As the storm surged around them, the crew and passengers threw one
thing after another off the ship to keep it afloat: first the cargo, then the
tools and navigational equipment, then the lifeboat and the last of their
food. Finally, even the anchors were cut.

In the midst of the stormy voyage, Paul had a dream that came from
God: the ship would be lost, but the crew and passengers, if they stuck

together, would be saved. With this encouragement, the occupants abandoned the ship on a rocky shoal off the coast of Malta, letting it be torn apart by the crashing surf; but they clung to its debris, and each other. Everyone was saved.

Ironically, this story of multiple losses is told in the context of the bigger story of the church in its first phase of dramatic growth and movement. As the crew and passengers cast aside all they had once believed was necessary to their journey, they relied more and more on the promise of God to move them forward. By letting go of everything but his faith, Paul was able to carry his most important cargo, the Good News, to Rome.

As you look back on your church's past, you can probably recall many things that have been "thrown overboard" through the years. But now, the winds of the Spirit are taking your church in a new direction, possibly even breaking it into something that is unnavigable. What precious cargo are you focused on passing on to future Christians?

CLOSURE AND DIASPORA

Many of the leaders I interviewed have already experienced the complete closure of their churches. They have sold their buildings and the members have dispersed or emigrated en masse to different congregations. These Christians have experienced the gradual loss of almost everything that gave them a place in thriving institutional churches. But at the end, they still had the Word of God and the blessed community of saints—those things that keep the church alive in every place and time. Their task was to relinquish the institutions they had fostered back to God's care and control, and many found ways to do this faithfully.

If closure is the decision you are led to, that decision will be the first of a series of important steps you will need to take to complete your ministry with due diligence. Faithful closure will be your new mission.

At this point, your church's by-laws should be consulted, as they may contain a dissolution clause stating how a decision to close can be enacted and/or what entity may lay claim to assets resulting from the dissolution.[1] Your judicatory office should be able to provide you with a list of legal and

---

1. See Additional Resources for an example of a dissolution clause used in the Unitarian Universalist Association of Congregations

ecclesiastical procedures your congregation will need to carry out in order to formally dissolve your church.[2] These may include

- a vote by your governing board and/or a regional body that affirms the decision to close by following appropriate local and denominational procedures,

- legal action, such as dissolving your nonprofit status according to state statutes,

- addressing property issues, such as the inventory of all church assets, cleaning, repairs and appraisal,

- sale of a building or transfer of ownership to another nonprofit entity,

- Dispersing emotion-laden "sacred objects" (these may include anything from baptismal fonts and stained glass windows to mixing bowls from the church's kitchen),

- Financial transactions, such as settling all debts and transferring endowments and bequests to new nonprofit entities.

Keep in mind that state statutes vary in regard to dissolving a nonprofit organization and dispersing its assets. Your denomination should be able to guide you to an attorney knowledgeable about church law.

ENTRUSTING GOD'S GIFTS

Most churches recall stories about accepting gifts from well-meaning members that were not . . . uh . . . appreciated. That burnt orange couch in the church parlor, for example. Others may remember times when the church entrusted a gift to someone else, only to see it misused.

If your building or its contents are sold, you as the seller will probably relinquish all rights to control how it is used by the buyer.[3] For example, one church sold its building to an evangelical new church development, relieved that the contents would continue to be used for sacred purposes. But as soon as the sale was completed, they watched in horror as the new owners dismantled the beloved pipe organ and threw it in the dumpster.

However, if church assets are *given* to another church or nonprofit, you can establish some reasonable guidelines as to how the assets will be

2. See Appendix B for a Presbyterian example of a checklist.

3. An exception would be when real estate has deed restrictions or easements attached to it.

used. One possibility is to draft a Memorandum of Agreement (MOA) with the party receiving your legacy, as a way of stating in writing how your church wishes the asset to be used.

Church assets that have significant monetary value cannot be given to individuals but must be transferred to another nonprofit organization or church. Wayne was a trustee at the time his church closed. His congregation felt beholden to return various objects given to the church back to their original donors. But this was an error in judgment. In fact, gifts given to your church in the past were just that: *gifts*. In many cases, the givers received tax benefits when the gifts were given. These objects were *given*, not lent, for the glory of God, so it is not appropriate, nor is it legal, to return them to the original donors.[4]

As you make decisions about who will receive your legacies, keep the designated use of the gift general; a congregation that tightly restricts the use of its legacy may prevent the *donee* (the party receiving the gift) from using it to accomplish needed ministries. For its part, the donee has a legal obligation to use a gift according to agreed-upon specifications.

How will your congregation disperse the church's contents, such as furnishings and art? Some churches sell or auction off these objects. Still others seek neighbor churches that will use them in the future. In chapter 10, you will read about different ways churches disperse objects of *sentimental* value to members of the congregation as part of the grief process.

Dr. Jane Heckles, who has served on the national staff of the UCC's Local Church Ministries, initiated the UCC's Legacy Church Project, which advises churches on pastoral and fiduciary issues when they are in the process of closure. "We feel that for churches to end their corporate ministry, in order to experience resurrection, they need to think through what they want to accomplish," she said. Heckles has developed resources to help guide churches in planning so that they don't just "drive up and hand over the keys" of their churches to their conferences. Instead, she advises them to consider and plan for how they want the legacies of their ministry to be carried on.

One vehicle for reinvesting in future ministry is through a legacy trust. In the UCC, according to Heckles, a property trust can be set up to allow a larger regional body (such as a conference or the UCC's United Church

---

4. The way your church initially received a gift will impact how you are allowed to disperse it upon closure. Consult your attorney or regional pastor about legal and practical ways of dispersing items that have monetary value.

Fund) to hold the deed to a defunct church's property as trustee and exercise the church's intent for its legacy gift. The trust may fund any nonprofit organization the former church chooses. As with personal trust funds, a legacy trust is legally bound by whatever terms are set by the donor. This allows a congregation to set mission goals for the use of its assets after the church is closed, with assurance that their wishes will be carried out.[5]

Your church is made up of many different kinds of assets, including property and financial assets, but also the spiritual gifts of members, the social capital you offer to your community as a gathering place, and the unique theological heritage you offer to Christians in your neighborhood. Below are a few stories of churches that closed and passed on their assets. As you read them, consider how your church's assets might be entrusted to the future.

DONATING PROPERTY FOR A NEW CHURCH DEVELOPMENT

June told me how many Caucasian families moved out of her neighborhood in the 1970s as African Americans were moving in. At her church, Immanuel, about half the Caucasian members continued to commute back on Sunday mornings for church, but the other half stopped coming. Meanwhile, only a few new black families were attracted to the church.

Eventually the membership got down to about forty-five worshippers on Sundays. Although the congregation hired an African American pastor in an effort to reach out to new neighbors, it was too little, too late. "Almost instantly [paying the salary] became a financial burden," June said.

The congregation and pastor parted ways and the church reached a crisis moment when they found they had only two months of reserve funds left to operate. At about that time, their conference minister told them about a large African American church in a nearby city that was looking to begin a satellite ministry. June and her conference minister began negotiations with that church, and Immanuel agreed to entrust the keys to their building to the conference in hopes that a new church could be developed on the site.

Shortly after June's church closed its doors, Immanuel UCC became New Vision UCC and began as a new church development serving the

5. A UCC *Legacy Church Workbook* is scheduled to be published by Local Church Ministries in 2013.

African American community with a progressive Christian faith tradition that makes it unique among black churches in its city. A trained pastor from the parent church was financially supported for a few years to get the ministry underway. While the new church inherited some of the same structural burdens of the building their predecessor dealt with, they are made up of an entirely new congregation, with an outreach to progressive African American Christians.[6]

CONVERSION OF A BUILDING TO NEW MISSION USE

Many of my interviewees reported feeling deep relief when their buildings were sold or given to another church for sacred use. But sometimes, other types of ministry can be housed in former church buildings.

St. John's Presbyterian was located in an urban area that experienced rapid demographic and ethnic change over a couple of decades. After a long-term supply pastor retired, they experienced a crisis of leadership. Gary, their executive presbyter (EP), stepped in.

The presbytery helped them find a transitional pastor, and an administrative commission helped them reach a decision to close their doors. Meanwhile, Hope Church, a young African American congregation in the same presbytery, was eyeing St. John's building with a vision in mind: to use the space for a community food pantry. Before the closure, St. John's had not been willing to consider a shared arrangement with Hope Church. But after the closure, the presbytery assisted Hope Church in acquiring the building and receiving grant funding to do extensive repairs.[7]

Gary reflected, "It wasn't their intention to give property away to [Hope Church], but in the end that's what happened. The leadership of the presbytery all saw that [St. John's] was going to close. We were hoping to do something. Was this a way to assist another church?" Hope Church went on to convert the St. John's building into a community food pantry, and a year later, they partnered with a medical clinic that treats chronic disease for pantry patrons.

6. One concern when transferring ownership of a building to a young congregation is the condition of the building. If your building needs extensive repair, it may prove to be more liability than asset to a fragile new church start.

7. The grant funding available to this church came from previous churches that had closed and given portions of their assets to their presbytery for use in new ministry ventures.

Many churches sell their buildings to secular organizations. The proceeds of the sale then become the asset that is passed on for future ministry ventures. The buildings may also go on to be valuable assets to their communities. In chapter 11, you will read about two secular organizations that added social capital to their neighborhoods after they purchased abandoned church buildings.

SOUL REVIVAL

The spiritual energy released by the closure of a church is not just given to new church developments or mission projects. It can also result in revitalized energy among former members of a closed church who move on to new ministries.

Remember Diane in chapters 3 and 4? She worked for years to help her congregation become more creative and responsive to community needs. But over and over, her efforts fell flat. The congregation was mired in division and fear, and she had few allies besides the choir director and an interim pastor. Finally, she stood up in worship one Sunday and announced her intention to leave the congregation because she could no longer practice her ministry with them in this toxic setting. Soon after, her interim pastor and music director also announced their departures.

Today Diane, her former interim pastor, *and* her choir director are all members of Pilgrim Church, located in a nearby neighborhood. Diane speaks with joy of the work she does with her new congregation. She has been able to practice her faith in ways that are life-giving for her and her community. This is a vast improvement over the years she spent in frustration in a system stuck in neutral.

After eleven years leading my own congregation, I was asked to resign when my church was on the brink of closure. As much as I wanted to stay and see them through the closure, it was clear that my departure was necessary before the congregation could face its future. God asked me to let go. Looking ahead at the prospect of leaving a "failed" ministry, not to mention unemployment, I went through a period of deep sadness and a sense of being humiliated by failure.

But a door opened for me that same year. It was an idea: to gather the stories of clergy and lay people who had experienced the closure of a church and compile them into a book. That idea became the book you are now reading. I felt that my church's difficult journey could benefit others who are walking a similar path. After leaving employment, God offered me time, space, and grant funding to take on research and writing that never would have been possible had I not been willing to let go of my pastoral position.

These examples illustrate how new opportunities can emerge from the closure of a church when faithful members are willing to let go of control, allow old forms to die, and let new ministries be born. These transformations occur because someone in the system is proactive and positive about accepting radical change and seeking out new opportunities for ministry instead of focusing on what has been lost.

HOW CAN YOUR MINISTRY BE RESURRECTED?

The options above, along with others in this book, are among the many that congregations have pursued in passing on their legacies. This kind of relinquishment entails an attitude of generosity and gratitude. Your congregation must ground itself in faith that everything you were given by life in your church was a gift from God and is owed back to God.

How about having a conversation at your church that includes dreaming of how your spiritual and financial assets can be passed on to do God's work? This will give hope and spiritual consolation to your members. Here are just a few ideas:

- Your building may be shared, sold, rented, or given to a new church development or nonprofit that is looking for space.

- Financial assets gleaned from a property sale may be used to assist new church development projects in your city or region.

- Church members can offer new vitality to the churches they move to by bringing with them a "spiritual gift inventory."

- Your church's theological heritage can be carried forward in ways that reach new populations (for example, by funding a campus ministry, an outdoor ministry, theological education, or a chaplaincy).

- There may be particular community needs that your congregation has a heart for. Maybe because of depleting energy, you were unable to address those needs in the past. But now, with the church's financial assets liquidated, you can give an existing nonprofit organization or another church the power to address them.

WHY PASS IT ON?

Churches that seek resurrection amid the ashes should ask themselves why any aspect of their ministry *should* be resurrected in a new form. What unique mission have you fulfilled that is worthy of being passed on? What precious cargo has God entrusted to you and asked you to carry to new shores? If your church's mission efforts are worth preserving, perhaps other neighboring churches, a charitable foundation, or your denomination will partner with you, offering dollars, prayers, and leadership expertise. Remember that, when considering how your congregation might allocate its assets, it is wise to work with the appropriate administrative body in your denomination for guidance.

Many mainline denominations are eagerly seeking to develop new churches and other mission ventures. They understand that such ventures are not financially self-sustainable in their early years. If you have an idea for funding a new ministry that might grow out of your church's closure, find partners who are excited about it and team up with them for support.

But remember, resurrection can only happen if something is allowed to die. An attempt at a new ministry that is really just designed to support the old one will not lead to rebirth. Whatever the options your group considers, congregations must ask not, "How will it still be *our* church (or "*our* money")?" but "How will it be *Christ's* church—resurrected?

God has ways of resurrecting the church that we cannot always see. Your assets may be transformed from simply keeping the building heated to sheltering homeless families, improving your beloved church camp, or building a school for girls in Pakistan. God doesn't waste any resource, and whatever your congregation lets go of in faith can be used by God to continue the building of Christ's reign. A decision to faithfully dissolve the ministry may be the most faithful decision you can make for God's purpose. While there is sorrow in letting go of the past, planning now for your church's closure will allow you pass on your legacy in faithful ways that give hope to emerging ministries.

REFLECTION

But now I urge you to keep up your courage,
because not one of you will be lost; only the ship will be destroyed.

ACTS 27:22

- With a group, read together the account of Paul's shipwreck in Acts 27 and 28. List together the objects mentioned that were thrown overboard and the various ways the crew lost control of their destiny. Then go back and list those events that offered hope and survival to the crew.

- Now list those things your congregation has given up along the way, and list the hopes that you still cling to.

- In Acts 28:30 we hear that Paul was active as an evangelist on the island of Malta, where the crew finally landed. What future mission endeavors might be possible using legacies your church provides?

10

Seven Ways to Say Good-Bye

I glorified you on earth by finishing the work that you gave me to do.
JOHN 17:4

AS A PASTOR, I'VE been blessed to be present with families as they walk through the valley of death and plan a funeral. During that time, the family has clear duties to perform, such as holding vigil at a bedside, conferring with funeral directors, and gathering the family. Later, there may be a home to clean out, and the legal work of executing a will. These tasks, while full of sorrow, give order to the chaos of mourning a death.

After the funeral, we express our grief in more personal and varied ways. Some will need privacy, while others crave social connection. Some people eat, while others fast. Some cry, and some feel a weight has been lifted. But over time, we let go of our "love objects." Memories are accumulated, meaning is attached to our losses, and new life practices are formed. We move on, changed forever by our experiences of grief.

Similarly, congregations need to mourn the death of their churches. But we don't have established ways to do so. Each church and regional body must create ways to attend to the sorrow that comes with ending a ministry.

In this chapter, we will explore how Jesus, at the end of his earthly life, let go of his earthly ministry and entrusted it to God and his disciples. His example models for us some healthy ways to complete a ministry.

JESUS' MODEL OF RELINQUISHING

Jesus' last hours give us a model of what Christlike relinquishment looks like. In those hours, he prayed for the unity of his disciples. He expressed faith in God's plan and acknowledged that he had completed his ministry on earth. But his walk to the cross was not a smooth path of acceptance. He had moments of doubt and fear. In the garden of Gethsemane, he asked God to "take this cup away from me" (Luke 22:42). But when violence erupted and the disciples prepared for a fight, he interrupted the tension with an act of healing. Throughout his ordeal, Jesus maintained his belief in God's saving power and never cut others off in anger or despair. He lived out his full humanness as far as the cross.

As you consider the end of your ministry in a local church, how can church members pursue this full humanity modeled by Jesus? Tradition tells of Jesus' seven last messages uttered from the cross. These messages, spread throughout the four gospels, reflect both his agony and his hope for the future. Consider what these phrases have to offer your congregation in the closure process.

"FATHER, FORGIVE THEM, FOR THEY DO NOT KNOW WHAT THEY ARE DOING"

Jesus had many people to forgive: the disciples who abandoned him, the Jewish leaders who set him up for failure, the Romans who tortured him, and the bandits hanging by his side. Even on the cross, his arms were open wide enough to accept anyone who wished to be reconciled with him.

Forgiveness is perhaps the first spiritual task necessary for Christians who wish to complete a ministry with gratitude. Declining congregations may have experienced years of anger and shame about their own decline.

Forgiveness Among Factions

Forgiveness may be required between different factions of the church. For example, one group may have pushed for a geographic move, while another voted to close. Once a decision is made, spiritual leaders of the church should enact rituals of reconciliation, and new roles and duties should be placed before the congregation to help unify the group as it pursues the tasks of closure.

Forgiveness Between Pastor and Congregation

No matter how long the decline has been occurring, the pastor in place at the time of closure will bear some measure of blame, whether deserved or not. Pastors are blamed for staying too long, or not long enough, for being too conservative or liberal, too controlling, or for being a "church killer."

Your pastor may need to be forgiven for a lack of professionalism or for being inexperienced in dealing with decline. No pastor is perfect. The congregation must come to terms with the multiple reasons why the ministry is now ending and put aside blame. In my own ministry, I found it helpful when one trusted leader came to my office and said, "You cannot take responsibility for everything that has happened here." Those words gave me comfort when many members silently withdrew from me.

In the same way, the pastor may need to offer mercy to a congregation that did not fulfill his/her expectations. After years of viewing my own church as a set of problems to be solved rather than a group of people to be loved, it was not easy to shift from blame to forgiveness. To help accomplish this, I worked with a spiritual director who had a background in family systems. As I expressed my frustration and anger with my congregation and myself, she challenged my assumptions and supported my best instincts. This guidance was invaluable in the months leading up to my departure, as it allowed me to step away from the role of "fixing" the church and lean into loving them with more compassion and patience.

In some cases, congregations need to seek reconciliation with regional pastors. Recall from chapter 6 that these leaders also have their limits. While your regional pastor wants to help you through discernment and transition, he or she may not have the time or experience to closely guide your congregation. When tension surfaces between a congregation and denominational staff, take time to talk together honestly. Each party should be able to share what they have learned from the process and what could be done differently next time. Local congregations have nothing to lose by honestly sharing their feelings about a closure, and a regional pastor who allows his/her own vulnerability to be a part of the process has a much better chance of healing any discord that may occur. While closure conversations may take time, they are well worth it if they prevent long-term bitterness and even lawsuits between denominational bodies and their churches.

Forgiving the World

As the pastor of a dying church, a thought often festered in the back of my mind: If only those old members hadn't left. If only those inactive members would come back. Then we would still be strong.

But at a certain point, I had to forgive the world for not being what it once was. I was finally helped by having time to visit other churches during a sabbatical. I saw that some of these churches were declining as mine was, while others were strong and vibrant. Each congregation had its own unique set of circumstances. Broadening my worldview in this way made it easier to forgive those who had left my little church. I could not know all the reasons they had done so. But, like Jesus' disciples, I had to brush off my feet and move on.

Rituals of reconciliation may be enacted in formal or informal ways. Michael Weldon, researching Catholic consolidations, found that, when hierarchical processes short-circuited the emotions and insights of the laity, reconciliation was difficult and long-standing resentment was the result. With more open conversation and rituals of reconciliation, members were helped to let go and move on in hopeful ways.[1]

Lucille was opposed to her church's decision to close, but she was able to move past her resentment when a matriarch of the church passed away. The congregation had long since ceased offering funeral lunches, because no one had the energy to prepare them anymore. But this funeral was special, and Lucille stepped forward to insist there would be a proper funeral lunch held at the church. She made sure everyone brought salads and desserts. Tables were set up, coffee was made, and the family of the deceased "came through" with purchased chicken. Everything was done right, and on the day of the funeral the church was packed.

"It meant the world to me," she says. "She was important to that church and this was my good-bye to her. I had to do it for me and for her." But Lucille also did it for her congregation, who used the occasion as a day of reconciliation and remembering. One week later, the church was closed.

Leaders can use seasons and events in the church year to help members live out their forgiveness, formally or informally. And Weldon advises that special rituals be created for various stages of a closure process, such as when members engage in prayerful conversation about the future, when

1. Weldon, *A Struggle for Holy Ground.*

a church is formally closed, when a building is vacated, and when a new ministry partnership (such as a merger) is initiated.[2]

What do members of your congregation have to forgive before they can complete a ministry that honors a merciful God?

"I THIRST"

John's gospel tells us that, on the cross, Jesus said "I am thirsty" (John 19:28). While he was always attentive to the needs of those around him, he did not ignore his own need.

At a time of grief, some people will focus exclusively on their own needs and become greedy for those services the church has always provided. For example, in one church, a fringe member demanded the church stay open so her relatives could be buried there.

But other members may give and give until they collapse from exhaustion. At Pastor Mark's church, a significant burden was placed on one lay leader, who did most of the church's financial and maintenance work. He finally resigned from leadership in order to stop propping up the system and allowed the closure to progress.

Congregations should be aware that, modeling Jesus, we start by considering the needs of others, but we do not neglect our own needs. This attitude of compassion for others and the self will shift the conversation about closure in a new direction when we ask:

- How can we all be cared for spiritually?
- Who in the community will be affected by a closure, and what are their needs?
- And finally, what are my spiritual needs?

Remember that there may be members whose spiritual needs are no longer being met because of the strain of church decline. Having members identify their spiritual needs may reveal this, and help the group affirm its decision to pursue radical change.

The needs of various groups in the church may include, among others:

- The needs of vulnerable members for pastoral care and belonging
- The needs of children and youth for youth programming

2. Ibid.,, 149; see also sample liturgies that could be adapted for Protestant use, 197–235.

- The needs of lay leaders who wish to step down after years of devoted service

- The needs of the wider community for physical space or volunteer energy

- The needs of old friends to maintain their spiritual friendships

- The needs of the community for your denomination's unique theological witness

In a compassionate environment where all can share what they need, others will be invited to give as well as receive care from the group. Attempts should be made to satisfy the thirst of all who ask for living water.

What are members of your congregation spiritually thirsty for?

"MY GOD, WHY HAVE YOU FORSAKEN ME?"

When Christians hear Jesus on the cross quoting from the 22nd Psalm of lament, we hear a paradox of our faith: Jesus experienced true despair on the cross, but his lament came from a deep confidence in God's ultimate love and justice. Christian lament does not result in a broken relationship with God; it is an emotional expression *within* that relationship.

We believe that God did *not* abandon Jesus, even though he felt abandoned on the cross. This knowledge reminds us that, in our times of feeling abandoned, God is still present in the silence. God never gives up on us.

The expression of sorrow and lament is a necessary part of mourning. Lament before God is an expression of faith because it gives voice to our feelings and allows us to be heard by God. In the contemporary church, with its focus on praise, miracles, and silver linings, we are hard-pressed to find resources for lament. But the scriptures are full of them. The Psalms and Lamentations offer laments that express:

- our complaints to God

- our appeal for God's intervention

- our remembrance of ways God has saved us in the past

- our trust that God will continue to offer salvation

Weldon offers an example of a ritual in which a congregation writes or names their losses and grief out loud, followed by silent reflection. After that, everyone names "some newness or joy" the congregation has experienced in its transition. This, he says, allows the group to give voice to their grief, while also inviting them to see beyond the grief to present blessings and future hope.[3]

Jaco Hamman, in his book *When Steeples Cry*, recommends giving members the chance to write their own laments, based on their personal experience.[4] These could be used in worship at a time of confession and assurance. During Lent, lament texts can be the basis of sermons. Hymns of lament in our hymnals, which are sparsely used, can be brought out for singing and reflection. If a group experience of lament is not possible, invite people in personal visits to express their laments to a pastor or lay visitor. These could be recorded and shared in liturgical settings, artwork, or original music.

A pastor or lay leader may lead a ritual that honors memories the congregation is grateful for. For example, the group might walk through the church building and talk about memories in each room, offering a prayer of blessing to the space. Rituals like these give spiritual focus to the real discernment, division, and grief a congregation may encounter on its way to closure.

In my own church, the period of lament began for me when I was able to say at a meeting, "I miss Rita and John and Elizabeth. . . . " I said out loud the names of member who had once been active and were now gone. That night, no one responded to my lament. I realized I was in a different stage of grief than others in the congregation.

But a few months later, members of the session entered their own period of mourning when someone at a meeting said, "I remember when. . . ." and members began talking about how the church had changed. Unlike previous conversations, no one stepped in to "save" the church by saying, "We just need a few more members and everything will be back to normal." Only when the congregation was willing to talk about its sorrow were they able to begin planning for a change in course for their future.

What sorrow do you have to bring to God? Where in the gathered community can you express that sorrow?

---

3. Ibid, 157–58.
4. Hamman, *When Steeples Cry*, 123–134.

"TODAY YOU WILL BE WITH ME IN PARADISE"

In the midst of his suffering on the cross, Jesus found himself in the company of two robbers who were also being crucified. When the repentant robber asked Jesus to remember him "when you come into your Kingdom," Jesus spoke prophetically of "paradise," a place where they would be together—that very day (Luke 23:42).

Was Jesus talking about heaven? One presumes so, but Jesus often reminded his followers that the Kingdom was not just a place in the future or in the sky; it was a state of being in the present. "The Kingdom of God has come near to you," he said in Luke 10:9. Clearly, whatever Jesus was referring to, it was a time and place beyond their suffering, which he could see with the eyes of a prophet. Not only was Jesus envisioning the end of his own suffering, he was able to reach out and share his vision with a fellow traveler, imagining a place where there would be enough bread, healing, and love for everyone.

Grieving churches need to hear that God has a bigger and better vision for them than failure and death. It takes a prophetic voice to have the courage to say, "We can do better ministry than this if we let go and trust God." But that voice is needed if people are to let go of old models that are no longer serving God's purpose.

How can a dying congregation catch a vision of God's plan for paradise? Regardless of our current circumstances, Christians are encouraged to keep their eye on the hope of God and the Kingdom promise. Instead of focusing on what has "failed" in your church, take time to study and reflect on your accomplishments for God's reign in the past and present, and celebrate them.

Then, look forward: how might God continue that building in the future, and where is it already happening? Try walking the neighborhood together and finding ways God is already building a new reign out there, even now.

A vision of a paradise where the gifts of ministry will again be used in lively ways can apply not just to institutions but also to the individuals within your congregation. Each person should be encouraged to imagine their future ministry in a new setting and make their own spiritual inventory of gifts they want to share.

Finally, the Kingdom is not just something we look forward to in the future. It is something we experience in the present. Your congregation can practice being the church God is calling you to be *now*, in the midst of closure.

My own church, in its last struggling years, experimented in new ways with outreach to their neighborhood. We held a free ice cream social for neighbors in our parking lot. We hosted an AA group. We set up a display at the city's Gay Pride event. We became more connected to the community even in the midst of our decline. Although these efforts didn't save our church, they saved *us*. They helped us to redefine who we wanted to be as Christ's universal church in the world, even as our institutional life was ending.

At Riverview Church, the members gathered for a weekend retreat in their last year together, at which they focused on thanking each other for their ministry. They planned ways to celebrate their past so they could move forward in hope toward the future. And they left their old church bearing the assets of their past ministry, both financial and spiritual. In short, they grew in faithfulness as they prepared to close.

What is your image of God's Paradise? What from your church's historic ministry can you carry with you into that new place?

"DEAR WOMAN, HERE IS YOUR SON . . . . HERE IS YOUR MOTHER"

In John's Gospel, the first thing Jesus says after he is hung on the cross is addressed to his mother and his close friend: "Woman, here is your son," and to the disciple, "Here is your mother" (John 19:26–27). The disciple took Mary into his home and cared for her like his own mother from that time on.

Leading up to and even on the cross, Jesus helped people form spiritual families for nurture and support. He gathered the twelve disciples of varying social classes and made them one family. He sent the seventy out two by two, as missionary teams. No one in Jesus' circle was expected to "go it alone."

As congregations move toward closure, they should consider whether they will stay together or disperse. Both can be faithful ways of moving forward. Some congregations are kept strong by staying together and moving en masse to a new church. Other congregations have "family systems" in place that are actually diminishing the spiritual energy of some members.

For example, a dominating leader may continue to intimidate members in the new setting. In a case like that, it might be better for members to disperse to two or more congregations and spread their wings in new places.

While every member should find a new church home, some will prefer to take some time out before attaching to a new congregation. In my own setting, most members chose one of two other churches to begin attending immediately. But a few members were not emotionally ready to reattach. After being deeply committed to the struggling church that closed, they wanted some time for "Sabbath rest" from church affiliation before moving on to new church homes.

The dispersing of a congregation to different new churches is a special challenge. Pastor Don, who has worked with several small, rural churches, observes that preservation of relationships formed in a faith community is often the highest priority in a declining church. Members who are called to give up a building and pastor may not necessarily be willing to let go of one another. Opportunities for monthly fellowship, weekly Bible studies, memorial events, or reunions should be explored. Unfortunately, when stripped of a pastoral relationship and a sanctuary, programming and friendships, some members will simply stop going to church, unless encouraged to find a new setting *before* their church closes.

To avoid setting members adrift in the midst of closure, give special attention to their various needs and gifts:

- Some members want to perform vital ministry elsewhere: these members will benefit from a spiritual inventory of their own gifts, as mentioned above. Any new church your members migrate to can be asked to offer space for continued gatherings on occasion for a social event or anniversary service, if desired.

- Some members cannot move to a new church because of frailty: elderly or disabled members, and those living in group settings, may not be able to attach to a new pastor or travel to attend church in a new location. Your regional pastor can be asked to appoint an area pastor to continue visitation with homebound members. In two cases I observed, a pastor who had served the church before its closure was hired to continue homebound care. Another idea is to ask former members to form a lay-led care team to their own homebound members after the closure. It is essential that vulnerable members not be forgotten, even if they refuse to affiliate formally with a new congregation.

- Church staff: your pastor, secretary, organist, and custodian are part of your church and deserve careful consideration as you end your ministry. Be aware that they will also be grieving. They may be losing friendships, income, and benefits.

Wayne's congregation used the assets of its building sale for a reserve account that funded their pastor's salary for three years as they merged with another congregation. This allowed for both the needs of the pastor for employment, and the congregation, who wanted to keep their trusted leader throughout the merger transition.

In my own setting, things did not go so smoothly. After trimming my hours to cut costs, a few members pulled me aside one Sunday and asked me to resign, saying, "Gail, your skills no longer match our needs." While I recognized the time had come for significant change, I also knew my skill set was not the issue. My church's leaders had no language to begin a conversation about ending my ministry other than the cold, corporate lingo they were accustomed to in their own workplaces. Surely in the church, we can do better than that.

If and when a pastor must be laid off, it is preferable to have such decisions made by a conscientious team of leaders, including the pastor and a wider church representative, who agree on the right course of action in a transparent way. The reasons for a pastor's resignation should be shared as openly as possible with the congregation so there are no rumors of misconduct or inadequacy.[5] Remember that clergy cannot apply for unemployment compensation, so it is appropriate to negotiate a severance to assist a pastor with the transition.

While caring for individual members is an important component of a transition to closure, all parties should remember that the functions of a church can continue whether or not your group stays together, because each person carries the universal church within them.

Carla and her daughter Mallory were members of our church before it closed. Mallory was born with a condition that affected her appearance and speech, and she lived with a tracheotomy tube in her neck and a feeding tube in her stomach. Mallory was beloved by our small congregation and often walked among the grandmas and grandpas on Sunday mornings, greeting each one lovingly. She had learned among us that, even though

---

5. If pastoral misconduct is an issue, your regional body should assist you with the process of discipline and/or dissolving your relationship with your pastor.

some strangers were repelled by her appearance, the world is full of good people.

Because Mallory had a safe place in our congregation, members were concerned that, once the church closed, she might have difficulty being accepted in a new congregation. When Carla explained the concern for Mallory's future, I reflected for a moment and said, "No one has to worry about Mallory finding a new church. Mallory *is* the church. She takes the church with her wherever she goes. The rest of us need to follow her example."

As members plan for the dispersing of a church family, they can also look forward to forming new relationships that are life-giving and purposeful. You are missionaries, sent out by God, whether all together or two by two. Wherever you go, take the church with you!

Scan your church's membership list and consider the needs of each member and friend. How will you help each other meet your spiritual needs in the future?

"INTO YOUR HANDS I COMMEND MY SPIRIT"

When Jesus said these words (Luke 23:46), he was entrusting his whole self to God's care and purpose: his ministry, his body, and his spirit. This kind of ultimate trust in God's power is something that all Christians can aspire to.

Up to now, we have discussed the spiritual and emotional tasks of ending a ministry. But finally, we let go physically. At the funeral, the body of the deceased is often present for a viewing so that the disbelief of the community can be alleviated and the truth can sink in: this beloved human being is no longer living. *Let go of the body.* The actual separation from the physical presence of our beloved dead is probably the most painful moment in the grieving process. Those things we can physically touch keep us connected to a time when the dead still lived beside us.

In interviews I conducted, one of the greatest heartbreaks expressed was over loss of buildings that symbolized meaning in people's lives. Weddings, baptisms, and funerals, joyful youth gatherings, deep friendships, and community milestones were symbolically housed in churches and among sacred objects.

In Lucille's case, before I even turned on my tape recorder, she blurted out, "We were never told where the stuff in the church went to—the pews and cross and things. Maybe they're still in the church!" The way in which "the stuff" is handled contributes to the health or disease of the congregation as it relinquishes its life to God. Let's look at a few examples.

At Lucille's church "the stuff" was handled awkwardly. After the decision to close had been made, lay members were invited to a meeting to claim any objects their families had given.[6] Lucille didn't know of anything her family had given, but there was a painting she dearly loved: a copy of the classic Warner Sallman painting, "Christ at Heart's Door." She raised her hand and shyly asked, "Did anyone give that painting?" When no one claimed it, she said bravely, "Pastor, I want that." And it was given to her. The next Christmas her daughters had it reframed and it now hangs in her living room. The day she led me to see it, her eyes filled with tears as she told how she had acquired it.

Nevertheless, after Lucille's church closed, she was left with ambiguity as to what happened to the other "stuff": the pews, cross, font, and other sacred objects. This ambiguity haunted her; she told me she avoids driving by the empty church in her home town.

In a different dilemma, Immanuel Church was told to leave all the furnishings and sacred objects in the building for a new church development that would be taking possession of it. But months later, June, the church's moderator, received a frantic call from her regional pastor: the new church didn't want their old things, and they must be removed. In less than a week, she and two other former members cleaned their old church's interior, tossing cherished objects and reliving the grief of their goodbyes.

Dealing with those tangible memory-holders is delicate work. If possible, the entire congregation should participate as they are able. As with cleaning out a family home, the grief work is done as members comb through and recall all that has occurred in this place.[7]

Many churches have given sacred objects to other area churches. Some churches will hold an auction among the members to disperse objects that do not have sacred meaning. But at the tiny, rural, Rosalind Church, they were so emotionally connected to even their pots and pans that an auction seemed crass. When the time came to disperse the building's contents, the group held a congregational meeting to which fourteen members came. Someone had the idea to give each item to whoever was willing to tell a

---

6. I don't recommend this practice as it obscures the significance of giving a gift for the glory of God and may create legal problems. Refer back to chapter 9.

7. Your denomination may require that a complete inventory of church assets be listed and photographed.

story about why the object was meaningful to them. The pastor asked the group, "What happens if two people tell equally great stories about the same object?" There was a silence and then "one dear, sweet lady got a smirk on her face and said, 'Then we'll have to tell *more* stories!'" The giving away of sacred objects, along with the telling of sacred stories, was the last event the church celebrated together.

The spiritual task of relinquishing gifts requires our awareness that all we are given belongs first and foremost to God. Our gifts are not ours to keep, horde, entomb, or discard. They are *God's* possessions, lent to us for the furthering of God's Kingdom. Entrusting legacies to a future generation means trusting God to make the best use of them.

What objects in the church have the most meaning to your faith life? What is your dream for how God might use them in the future?

"IT IS FINISHED"

When my aging father could no longer handle his own affairs, we decided to clean out his house and make it available for rent. I flew home to pack up the family heirlooms. It was a focused, solitary week combing through all the physical objects that gave my father's life meaning. Listening to his jazz albums, combing through photos and letters he wrote from the Great War, I nestled his life in boxes. Many things went to Goodwill. But the heirlooms were loaded on a truck and taken to a storage facility. As the movers locked the padlock on the storage room door, I turned away to weep. There in that room were all the objects that had defined my father's life. Although he was still living, I knew a significant chapter of his life was now over.

Most churches will plan a closing worship service that honors their history and mission. One tradition includes the ritual removal of sacred objects such as the font, cross, and communion set, similar to the stripping of an altar on Good Friday. Your denomination may have specific liturgical resources for the dissolution of a church, or you can be creative in designing a service in which all can participate in recalling the miracles God has performed through your church and the ways the mission will continue in new forms.

Pastor Don told of the tiny, rural, Hutchins Presbyterian Church, which was reluctant to end its ministry because they valued their annual Christmas Eve celebrations together. But eventually the decision was made to give the building to a community tutoring program. At that point, "the session took on new life," said Pastor Don. "Having a use for the building was a huge relief. They didn't want it torn down or used to store corn." The members found their authority again and began to plan for the last Christmas Eve service, with a revered member reading the Christmas story out of the Bible, according to tradition. It was their last service together.

At Pastor Bob's urban Riverview Church, the last weekend of their ministry included the full day of worship and remembrance that you read about in chapter 8. But after everyone else went home, the session had a "happy hour." "About fifteen of us sat around and had a beer and talked as the delivery people came [to remove furnishings]," he said. As the movers walked by, one stopped and observed the leaders sitting around with their beers. He said, "If I'd known there was a church out there that gives beer at their meetings, I would have come." Everyone laughed. Riverview Church had not lost its sense of humor even on that difficult day.

In churches torn by shame or unarticulated grief, closing services may not be so positive. St. James Church had shrunk down to thirteen widows at the last. They resisted their presbytery's vote to close their doors at every stage. Loretta, their executive presbyter (EP), felt burned by their resistance and was no longer sympathetic to their concerns. The congregation scheduled their closing service on a Sunday morning, when other members of the presbytery and neighbor churches would not be able to attend. However, the EP and some of the administrative commission were there. Loretta later said, "There was nothing grace filled. They were always fighting against the presbytery. The last service was anger-filled. They had their dinner and walked away, and really it was giving the finger to the presbytery."

After the service, Loretta and some administrative commission members literally cleaned up the dishes and later took on the task of cleaning out the church's furnishings. (In chapter 11 you will read about how God transformed this story for a happy ending).

It is said that "we die the same way we have lived." There may be cases when the negative cloud of energy in a congregation before the closure will hover over it until its last days. All we can do in those cases is bury the dead and keep believing in resurrection.

When Jesus said "It is finished" (John 19:30), he left no room for doubt about the ending of his earthly ministry. He stopped breathing, and his body grew lifeless. He was wrapped in cloth and placed in a sealed grave. His followers could begin to grieve, knowing he had truly died.

It's different with churches. The building may still stand in the community, and members may still see each other in other churches or in the neighborhood. The loss is less tangible than the loss of a physical body. But for many members, the signs of resurrection will become apparent over time, as new ministry is lived out in new settings.

Jesus' prayer for his disciples in John's farewell discourse (John 17) points to what it means to complete a ministry with dignity and faith. The prayer is laced with concern and love for those left behind. But he also affirmed that he had completed the tasks God set before him and understood that the work of the church was just beginning. He let go, and he accepted the commendation of his God, who says to all disciples, "Well done, good and faithful servant" (Matthew 25:23, NIV).

Christians are called to live each day in the awareness that life is limited, and to trust God's hand in life and death. In these times of multiple losses, from stock market crashes to end-of-life issues, church leaders are wise to keep before their congregations the reality that the creation includes cycles of life and death, beginnings and endings, even as God leads us ever closer to the promised Kingdom.

REFLECTION

- With a group, discuss the seven messages of Christ and the questions accompanying each message. Which of these messages has your congregation responded to already? Which still need to be addressed?

- What occasions are you finding to act out forgiveness and share your church's sacred stories and objects?

- Write a prayer for your congregation in the manner of John 17 and say it together in public.

11

New Wine for New Wineskins

No one sews a piece of unshrunk cloth on an old cloak; otherwise, the patch pulls away from it, the new from the old, and a worse tear is made. And no one puts new wine into old wineskins; otherwise, the wine will burst the skins, and the wine is lost, and so are the skins; but one puts new wine into fresh wineskins.

LUKE 2:21–22 (NRSV)

I'VE MADE IT THROUGH my audition and nabbed a role as the Sugar Plum Fairy in the local community theater's production of *The Nutcracker*. To-night is the first rehearsal. Being a newcomer, I am quietly observant as I get a lay of the land among my fellow actors, most of whom are strangers to me.

There are the veteran actors who have secured their usual lead roles, most of them middle-aged and trailing children. They are sitting up front, gabbing or tinkering with props and costumes as they wait for rehearsal to begin. There's the director, a large man in his late twenties, quietly scanning the crowd, searching for his own authority. And there is a gaggle of teenag-ers in a back pew, gossiping and fingering their iPods.

Wait . . . the back pew?

Yes, we are seated in the pews of what was once St. Elizabeth Catholic Church, now retrofitted to stage theater productions. The old chancel has been transformed into a stage with a proscenium and heavy red curtain. Klieg lights are fixed to the ceiling. In the rear of the sanctuary, the confessional, now known as "The Concessional," has been refashioned with a window at which theater patrons can purchase soda, popcorn, candy, and beer. In each pew, the kneelers are still ready for use.

The Branch Community Theater is the brainchild of Brad and his Aunt Kathleen, who both loved theater and teamed up when Brad was a teenager to begin producing plays ten years ago. For the first few years, they rented the town hall, using a moveable stage and writing their own plays to avoid the cost of royalties. They eventually raised enough money to purchase the abandoned St. Elizabeth Catholic Church for $60,000, after a generous donor offered them a no-interest loan with a ten-year repayment plan.

Since its inception, the theater has been built entirely on volunteer sweat and donations, with everything from builders and set designers, costume makers and music directors chipping in for the effort. The result is a lively multiage arts organization that produces two musicals and a play each year using local talent, all in a small town of 1,900 residents.

You may remember Kris from chapters 3 and 10. She taught me that all of us are dying, but those who know they are dying have the opportunity to make peace with their mortality and live joyfully in the present. After she was diagnosed with cancer and had to give up her job as a nurse, Kris got involved in the theater, designing costumes and occasionally taking her place on stage in small roles next to her son. It was Kris who encouraged me to audition. In this performance of *The Nutcracker*, Kris will be joined by a menagerie of performers, including whole families with young children, latchkey teenagers, college kids, retirees, and one unemployed clergywoman.

The central figure is Brad, 28 years old and living his dream as the company's director, manager, and star performer. When asked what his primary mission is, he replies, laughing, "To be a star." And at heart, this is his truth: to find a life in the theater without leaving his little town, Brad had to create his own theater. His favorite characters to portray are female: a tall vixen in platform shoes or a grumpy old woman in housecoat and boots. In a town as small as this one, the "local boy makes good" story takes on an ironic spin when Brad emerges on stage in a feather boa. But he says the community's response to the theater is "all positive." Besides developing his own acting career, Brad is proud of the theater's ability to bring people together, get kids "off the street," and give them something positive to accomplish together.

In the months of rehearsal leading up to my first performance with the theater, I spend many hours hanging around the Green Room (the old sacristy behind the stage) and the sanctuary, now the theater's "house." And as time passes, it begins to feel more and more like a church. It houses a cast of characters that includes divas and janitors, lost souls and leaders, ticket takers and popcorn makers. Look around your church, and you will see something similar.

There are marked differences, of course. Instead of weekly worship as its "performance," the theater company spends three months preparing for a two-week run of each play. And unlike a church, with its youth groups, Sunday school, and senior activity groups, the cast at this theater is mercilessly intergenerational, with everyone from age five to sixty-five learning dance steps and song lyrics at roughly the same pace. Arthritis and teenage hormones flare up in the same tiny rooms backstage where actors apply makeup and make costume changes. When the performances are over, grownups gather at the Concessional's bar to taste each other's homemade wine, while teenagers turn up the volume on *Glee* CDs and dance on the stage.

There is no worship of God in the former St. Elizabeth Church, but performance has its own transcendent appeal. We lose ourselves in our characters, memorize the liturgy of our lines, and bond like family for a few weeks in the shadowed wings.

Some of the actors are churchgoers who rush home from Sunday services to change into costumes for matinee performances. Others have made the theater their primary social connection outside of work and family. The whole enterprise generates a lively web of relationships in a town that has lost two churches and a bank in the past decade.

Brad says it is common for former church members to enter the theater and recall weddings and baptisms held there. A few of these members have stepped up to volunteer at the theater, selling candy and cleaning floors after performances. The stained glass windows are now boarded up, but older folks recall which ones bore their family names. The building has its own rich history as a church, but now it has been infused with a new spirit and purpose that offers belonging and pride to its community in the present day.

INNOVA DESIGN

Innova Design, an advertising firm, sits in the heart of its small city: a turn-of-the-century brick building covered with ivy on its north face. Inside, a sleek, modern reception area faces an airy atrium that opens into two levels of small office spaces. An upstairs balcony overlooks the atrium on three sides. Through the atrium's east doors, one can see additional office space—computer screens flicker in a dimly lit room where young designers are working quietly.

Innova is a typical advertising agency in many ways, but there is something different about its interior. Look up and you will see a large, stained glass window to the north depicting a scene of Jesus standing by a door. John, the owner, points up at it and says, "We call this 'Jesus Trying to Get Into Studio 54.' But he'll never get in wearing those clothes!"

Innova is housed in the former St. James Church, which closed several years ago under a cloud of resentment (you may recall St. James Church from chapters 3 and 10). Its building was erected at the turn of the twentieth century, during the gilded age of church construction. After the presbytery voted to close the church's doors, it sat empty as buyers were pursued.

John, who is not only a business owner but active in the nonprofit community, toured the building after hearing about it from a friend. Many of its artifacts and windows were already marked for sale at a planned auction. The rumor was that a neighborhood bank wanted to buy the property and demolish the building to make room for a parking structure.

A lover of historic buildings, John was infatuated with the structure and obtained financing to purchase it, along with a small adjoining lot, for $275,000. He then borrowed another $880,000 to renovate and retrofit the space for offices.

But John wanted to do more than just create office space. His vision included repurposing everything he found inside. The balcony railings were left in place. The pews were disassembled and recycled as shelves in the basement to hold the business library. The organ pipes are being fashioned into an outdoor sculpture. And whenever there's a birthday, the offering plates are passed around to collect for birthday gifts.

John views Innova Designs as more than a business. It is his mission project. Employing the "80/20 rule," he explains that "80% of our business is for profit. This affords us the opportunity to do 20% of our projects for nonprofits." His ad agency has done free publicity for causes such as a local alcohol treatment program, a family shelter, and an AIDS walk.

In addition, John has made the property into something he calls a "community hub." He offers the atrium space for free to community groups for fund-raising events, small music productions, and weddings. He sees the space as being both sacred and secular, a place of welcome for people who may not be comfortable in traditional churches.

John was raised Catholic, but he gave up Catholicism as an adult and no longer attends church. Nevertheless, he has a spiritual gift of hospitality that has guided his life. He has always felt compassion toward the homeless and hopeless, and they seem to find him. Because the building is located downtown, homeless passers-by often stop in to use the bathroom, or ask for money or a ride. John usually tries to help. In one case, he shepherded a young man to enter a nearby drug treatment center he does advertising for. Many assume he is the minister of the "church," which has remained virtually unchanged on the exterior. "I don't go out of my way to say we're not a church," he says.

John confesses that the last few years have been rough financially, but he feels the twenty-year-old business has staying power. "I have thirty employees," he says, explaining his resolve to stay in business. "They're like my congregation. They have families."

The former St. James Church, a tangle of mission purposes severed from God's renewing Spirit, is now gone. But in its place, a dechurched business owner is fulfilling a vision to build lively social connections and reach out to those in need in the heart of his city.

ST. ANDREW'S PRESBYTERIAN CHURCH

St. Andrew's Presbyterian Church was formed in 1955 in what was then the outskirts of Tulsa, Oklahoma. The members met at two elementary schools before constructing their own building in 1960. After several decades at that location, the congregation decided its aging building no longer met their needs. Instead of engaging in expensive repair and remodeling, they decided they would rather focus more of their resources on mission. At about that time, they were approached by a nearby school for children with disabilities who offered to buy the building.

"When we were asked, the session did not say no—they said, 'Let's go to the next step and see where it goes from there,'" said the Rev. Ann LaMar. After the sale, they moved to another church building where they shared space with two other congregations. Each congregation maintained its own separate identity, but all three engaged in joint worship and other ministries. This partnership lasted three years before it was dissolved.

"We had talked about becoming a missional church," said LaMar. "So we purchased a house on an acre of land." They converted the garage into worship space and dubbed it "the Church House."

God has not stopped nudging the St. Andrew's community forward. Their new church house sits on an acre of land directly across the street from an apartment complex that is home to many at-risk youth. "One of our deacons looked out at the backyard and said, 'That would make a great community garden,'" said LaMar. "So, we started an outreach to the youth—they come and help in the garden and then they are able to take the produce home with them."

St. Andrew's adventurous, nomadic spirit is making it possible for them to stay attentive to the Holy Spirit's leading. Whether camping out at a school, sharing space with other churches, or opening a "church house" to neighborhood youth, the members of St. Andrew's have maintained a mission that is both vital and viable.[1]

WHAT IS THE CHURCH?

Early in his ministry, according to Mark's Gospel, Jesus defined himself as a unique presence in his community, in contrast with the religious leaders of temple Judaism. In Mark 2, Jesus went to Capernaum and proceeded to surprise the crowd with unorthodox forms of leadership and mission. While teaching in a house, he offered hospitality and healing to a man who was lowered through the roof because he could not get in through the door. He then offered forgiveness and healing to the man without the authority of a priest. He called a despised tax collector to join his inner circle and shared meals with a variety of supposed ne'er-do-wells. He broke Sabbath law by gleaning wheat instead of fasting as other ascetics might. In the midst of these events, Jesus told a parable about the need to put new wine into new wineskins. The new covenant he bore was going to require a new ark.

Not long after the Holy Spirit was poured out among Christ's followers at Pentecost (Acts 2), the Second Temple would be tragically destroyed by Nero's persecution. Jesus' "new wine," poured out for his followers, would be housed in the new wineskins created by the young church just in the nick of time. In the absence of the temple, the church would, by necessity,

1. Dunigan, "A Change of Scenery," para. 2–14 and author interview.

become a fluid community that could penetrate the hearts of Gentiles, put songs in the mouths of prisoners, and set sail to Rome on a ship with Paul.

In our time, the church's flexibility is being tested. Is the church today a building with a steeple? Is it a congregation that worships God together on Sunday mornings? Is it a group of people who study Jesus and practice living by his words? Yes and yes and yes. It is all these things, and it can be many more. The *form* of the future church may take many shapes, but its *functions* are established by the inheritance we have received from Christ.

The great architect Louis Sullivan once wrote:

> It is the pervading law of all things organic and inorganic, of all things physical and metaphysical, of all things human and all things superhuman, of all true manifestations of the head, of the heart, of the soul, that the life is recognizable in its expression, that form ever follows function. This is the law."[2]

As you look to the future *form* of your own church's ministry, keep in mind the historic *functions* Christ's church has served in the world and how your church expresses them:

- The church exists for the hearing and telling of stories; and not just any stories, but in particular, that one Good Story of salvation history. We need to rehearse that story's lines until we feel ourselves to be characters within it.

- The church exists to create a connection between people that is about more than the expedient exchange of goods and services. We need soul companions who recognize Christ in each other's features.

- The church exists as a place of worship; we worship God, not because God needs to be worshiped, but because we need to celebrate God's obvious greatness and face our obvious unworthiness in a place where there are others who are just as amazed about it all as we are.

- The church is an incubator of compassion that prepares us to care for the vulnerable souls and creatures God places before us. We are wired for compassion and justice, but we need to be constantly reshaped into communities of deeper caring.

- The church is the visible sign of an invisible reality. We all need evidence that there is an ultimate goodness and divine purpose undergirding our world. We need to stare into a glass darkly and glimpse a

2. Sullivan, "The Tall Office Building Artistically Considered," 403–409.

parallel universe, *a better country* of generosity and truth telling. The church, despite all its human foibles, gives us that momentary glimpse of Christ's reign.

As you consider these functions, ask yourself how your church is embodying them now. Then consider how you might express them in whatever new form God is leading you toward. I suspect that, as we move into the uncertain future of the institutional church, as we are called to unload the precious cargo of buildings and committee structures, mission projects and social capital, we will need to ask questions about form and function over and over again.

What constitutes legitimate ministry? Can it be denominational, ecumenical, or even secular? Can "church" happen on your computer? Or does it require a physically gathered community? Does it include multiple elements such as worship, service, education, fellowship, and administration, or can we call it "church" if we perform only one or two of these functions?

However we answer these questions in the future, we need to remember that this is God's project, not ours. Our job is to let go of some of the beloved structures and traditions that connected us to God in the past, and then to sew together new wineskins for God's new wine.

God is not shrinking the church. God is *expanding* the mission project that started with the dawn of creation and continued in Jesus Christ and his disciples in every generation. That project has been passed down to us from those who piled stones in the desert to the builders of the Second Temple and the Scottish abbeys. It has wound its way through urban Detroit and rural North Dakota, and it will not stop until it has led us all to a better country.

REFLECTION

All of these died in faith without having received the promises, but from a distance they saw and greeted them. They confessed that they were strangers and foreigners on the earth, for people who speak in this way make it clear that they are seeking a homeland. If they had been thinking of the land that they had left behind, they would have had opportunity to return. But as it is, they desire a better country, that is, a heavenly one. Therefore God is not ashamed to be called their God; indeed, he has prepared a city for them.

HEBREWS 12:13–16 (NRSV)

- Discuss what you consider to be functions of an authentic church. Which of these functions is your church expressing now in your fellowship? Which functions would you like to pursue in the future?

- Considering the functions of the church you discussed in the previous question, what form or forms can you imagine your church's ministry taking in the future?

- What is the next step you want to take toward that better country?

Appendix A

Guidelines for Congregations Considering Merger
with One or More Congregations and That Seek the
Financial Support of the Presbytery of Milwaukee

Approved by the Presbytery February 2011

*Consequently, you are no longer foreigners and aliens, but fellow
citizens with God's people and members of God's household, built on
the foundation of the apostles and prophets, with Christ Jesus himself
as the chief cornerstone. In him the whole building is joined together
and rises to become a holy temple in the Lord.*

(EPHESIANS 2:19–21)

We often identify our faith communities with the buildings that house them yet we affirm that ministry is more than the bricks and the mortar; Jesus alone is the cornerstone on which we build. Buildings may house our ministries but Jesus is always calling us out into the world. In other words, it's not about the building so much as it is about building up the body of Christ in whatever form is most effective.

And yet for a particular community of faith, for the individual church which lies nestled within the church universal, place is important—the communities in which we live and the buildings in which we gather: our church home and home base.

Appendix A

In recent years, many congregations are prayerfully discerning God's leading into the future, a discussion that often leads to questions about our church buildings—how to shift our form in order to better serve our function, what to do with our buildings as congregations consider merging or closing, how congregations can be more fluid while still providing a place to meet and minister in the name of Jesus.

The Council of the Presbytery of Milwaukee has been considering these questions alongside congregations and we have put together these guidelines in order to foster discussion, open up options and partner in new visions for individual congregations. These guidelines should not be considered new policy; but they may point us toward new possibilities as we together seek the leading of God's Holy Spirit.

BACKGROUND

Particular congregations may seek new life and renewed ministry through merger with other congregations. Such a merger most often involves two or more congregations joining to form a new entity with a new name, a new roll of members, new mission, and, perhaps, a new location for worship, fellowship and mission. Whatever conditions originally prompt interest in a possible merger, the primary rationale for successful mergers is not simply survival but mission.

The product of a particular merger of two or more congregations varies with the specifics of the congregations involved. For example, the congregation resulting from the merger of two or more PC (USA) congregations would be a PC (USA) congregation that is organized, functions, and is governed as any other PC (USA) congregation. However, mergers including PC (USA) congregations and congregations outside the PC (USA) may take the form of either federated or union congregations whose organization and governance will be determined by the polity of the denomination of the merging congregations. In either case, mergers may only be completed and the resulting new congregation welcomed into the presbytery with the consent of the presbytery.

It is expected that when two or more congregations merge, the resulting congregation will locate its life and worship in one church building, chosen for its soundness and suitability for ministry, and that the other church building(s) will be sold. Other possibilities include selling all or some of the properties of the merging congregations and buying, renting, or building another site for the new merged congregation. Ordinarily, the assets of a congregation stay with that congregation as long as it is in ministry. When congregations merge, although they form a new entity, they are considered to be continuing in ministry and their assets become the assets of the new entity.

The formation of any new congregation always carries with it both promise and risk, but mergers also carry a high level of complexity. Such things as custom, history, social networks, institutional practice, denominational loyalty, resources and staff all need to be carefully and pastorally engaged. To be successful, the formation of a congregation by merger must be undertaken with the same intentionality and attention to detail as a new church development.

PROPOSAL

Any approved costs including all contracts incurred by the merger process will be paid for by the Presbytery of Milwaukee Foundation and all reimbursements shall be returned to the Foundation. All contracts must be approved by COM.

Congregations in the Presbytery of Milwaukee that are considering merger and request the presbytery's financial assistance, will:

1) Identify working groups of not more than 5 members from each congregation that will meet regularly to study the feasibility and desirability of merger;

2) Contract with a consultant/coach (from a list of COM approved consultant/coaches) who will work with the congregations for at least six months, to facilitate the merger process.

3) Bring together a building assessment team of appropriate experts (architects, property managers, engineers, etc., approved by the COM) to assess the soundness and suitability for ministry of all the existing church buildings and to make a report to the congregation and COM.

   • So that the cost of qualified consultants, architects and engineers not be an impediment to the exploration of a possible merger, the Presbytery of Milwaukee agrees to pay the approved costs incurred in the employment of the consultant/coach, the building assessment team, and the COM advisor for their work in advance of the merger. When particular skills are required COM may contract with advisors who have competency in the identified areas of need.

4) Develop a strategic plan, with the help of the consultant/coach, which includes a five year operational plan, staffing plan, and financial plan;

5) Present the completed plans to the congregation and COM for approval before any decision is taken regarding merger;

6) If, after consideration of the reports and the strategic plan the congregations vote not to merge, the process will end.

7) If COM determines the plan is not feasible or sustainable, COM may require the participating congregations to revise and resubmit the plan.

8.) If the congregations vote to merge, they agree to employ the same or another, COM approved, consultant/coach for a period of at least one year to assist in "working the plan" that was developed in the six months prior to the congregations' votes.

- It is expected that the Presbytery will be reimbursed for any such expenditures, either at the time of the merger, from the financial resources of the new congregation, or at a later date, from the sale of the properties of the merging congregations.

- If the participating congregations decide not to merge, the costs of the consultant/coach, building assessment team, and the presbytery's advisor will be covered by the presbytery.

NOTE: COM Advisors are to be recruited, trained, and paid by the COM to be a guide between the merger team and consultant, and COM.

Appendix B

Winnebago Presbytery

OUTLINE FOR CHURCH CLOSURE ADMINISTRATIVE COMMISSION

1. **Administrative Commission**

   1.1   Originating Action and Purpose:

   1.2   Membership:

   The Commission consisted of seven members

   1.3   Meetings:

   [Minutes of all meetings attached.]

2. **Church Dissolution**

   2.1   Initial Request of the Church

   2.2   Session (local church) Action

   2.3   Presbytery (governing body) Action

   2.4   Final Service of Worship

   2.5   Dissolution of the Church as civil corporation

   2.6   Public notice of corporate dissolution in public paper of record

   2.7   Final Commission Report

3. Resolution of Membership

3.1   Membership List

The Commission reports the list of members of the Church at the time of closure or dissolution.

3.2   Letter to Members

The Commission reports that each of the remaining members received a letter encouraging transfer of church membership and providing for the reporting of their wishes.

3.3   Transfer Requests

The Commission reports requests for transfer received from the following member[s]:

The Commission reports those members who remain as miscellaneous members of Presbytery or governing body, pending transfer to a local congregation:

3.4   Provision for Continuing Pastoral Care

The Commission may recommend:

- That Presbytery provide pastoral care and services to the untransferred members of the former Church until that time when all of the members have been transferred to other local congregations or all are deceased;

- That [name & title] be initially employed by the Presbytery to provide such pastoral care and services to these members from the former Church, according to contractual terms as arranged by the Committee on Ministry; thereafter, pastoral care and services are to be arranged by the Committee on Ministry;

- That the Clerk is to report annually those persons from the former Church who have not transferred membership to a local church and remain as miscellaneous members of Presbytery.

4. **Church Property**

    4.1   Real Property of the Church

         [Summary listing of the physical property of the Church at the time of dissolution]

         Appraisal Report

         The Commission solicits a professional appraisal of the church building and site. The appraiser's report evaluates a number of elements, e.g., location, restrictions, market conditions, conditions of the building, and include any specific assessments.

         [attach report]

    4.2   Legal Description:

         The legal description of the property is as follows:

    4.3   Title Search for Reversionary Clause

    4.4   Report on Sale

    4.5   Use of Sale Proceeds

         [The Commission may be authorized to dispose of the proceeds by its own action or it may recommend that the matter of appropriate use of sale proceeds be referred to the Finance Committee for recommendation to the presbytery or governing body or for action directly by presbytery or governing body.]

    4.6   Removal of Church symbols

         The Commission determines that all portable or detachable symbols related to the Church or to the Presbyterian Church (U.S.A.) have been removed and appropriately disposed, as follows:

    4.7   Continuity of Insurance and Claims report

         The Commission maintains full insurance coverage on the property until sale or disposal and determines that there are no outstanding claims.

         [Policy specifics]

    4.8   Equipment & Furnishings

The disposal record of other equipment and furnishings of the Church:

[listing of significant items]

    4.9   Cemetery

The Commission establishes the following provision for the perpetual care requirement if there is a cemetery portion of the property. [This will require a close examination of state law and possibly considerable legal expense if there is a transfer to a municipality.]

5. Other Property/Assets

    5.1   Final Financial Report

The Commission prepares and submits the final financial report[s]. [Appendices]

    5.2   Remaining Funds:

The final balance of church funds was _____.

[summary of various funds may be advisable]

    5.3   Continuing Financial Obligations to Presbytery

    5.4   Use of Fund balances [listing]

    5.5   Annuity or Endowment Continuances

[Annuity accounts or continuing endowment funds.]

    5.6   Determination of bequests or memorials that have continuing effect.

[certify that no bequests, funds or memorial provisions require assumption by Presbytery or governing body.]

6. Church Records

    6.1   Register of Membership

The Session Register of Church members to be archived.

6.2   Session Minutes

The Commission lists the record of Session (or church) Minutes

[listing of dates, volume designations, location]

6.3   Disposition of Records

The Commission provides for the disposition of the Church records

[Convey to the Stated Clerk of Presbytery or directly to the History Department and Archives of the Presbyterian Church (U.S.A.) in Philadelphia or other equivalent archival depository].

[Listing]

7.   **Final Reports**

7.1   Report to Presbytery

The Commission's final report is this report: [date]

7.2   Report to the Office of the General Assembly

The Clerk reports the dissolution of the Church to the Office of the General Assembly.

7.3   Report to the Synod

The Clerk reports the dissolution of the Church to the Synod.

7.4   Presbytery Permanent Minutes

The Permanent Minutes of Presbytery is to contain this report in full.

Revision for public distribution August 2013

Appendix C

Services from the Massachusetts Conference, U.C.C. for Member Churches considering closure

1. **Pastoral Care**: The regional Associate Conference Minister is available to provide appropriate pastoral care to both clergy and laity of member churches, including assistance with planning final celebration and worship services. In the event the pastor leaves prior to closing, the Conference will assist in obtaining interim pastoral coverage.

2. **Advice, Counsel and Referrals**: Mass. Conference staff, including the regional Associate Conference Minister and the Associate Conference Minister for Stewardship & Financial Development are available to meet with pastors and lay leaders to discuss the various considerations and steps involved in church closings, including issues of continuing legacy and legal options and requirements.

3. **Legacy Services**: Churches may continue their legacy by nurturing local church vitality and the covenant among our churches through distribution of some or all of their remaining financial assets to one of several Conference Funds:

    a. Pastoral Excellence Endowment Fund

        This endowment fund provides income for ongoing support of the Pastoral Excellence Program of the Massachusetts Conference. Income from the Fund may be used to support Conference programming designed to promote pastoral excellence by pastors holding standing in the Massachusetts Conference. Currently this programming includes continuing education events, New Clergy Groups and Clergy Communities of Practice.

b. Justice and Witness Fund

This fund supports the Mission and Justice ministries of both the Conference and the congregations of the Massachusetts Conference. Funds may be used for Barnes grants to congregations, support of Mission & Justice task teams, programming and resources.

c. 21st Century Congregations Fund

This fund assists churches to successfully meet the challenges of ministry in the context of contemporary society. Funds may be used for programming, coaching, consulting, training and grants to support local church transformation, missional effectiveness, lay leadership development and long-term vitality.

d. Seeds of Faith Fund

This fund promotes faith development within the Massachusetts Conference. Funds may be used to provide programming, resources and grants to local congregations to support faith, generosity and discipleship formation of children, youth and adults. Funds may also be used to support programming and/or resources by the Conference for faith development of individuals [e.g.—on-line bible studies, spiritual retreats, etc.].

e. General Endowment Fund

This fund provides support for all the services and programs of the Massachusetts Conference.

The above funds represent a comprehensive list of choices for churches to give to the mission and ministry of the Massachusetts Conference, as it carries out its mission to nurture local church vitality and the covenant among our churches to make God's love and justice real.

f. Named Funds

For legacy gifts of $500,000 or more the Conference will create a new permanent endowment fund, named in memory of your congregation. A provision should be made for how the fund would be used in the event the named purpose becomes impossible or impractical to fulfill.

For legacy gifts of $50,000 or more the Conference will create a named expendable fund in memory of your congregation.

In either case, the purpose of the fund must be consistent with the purpose of the Conference to nurture local church vitality and the covenant among our churches, and be accepted by the Conference Board of Directors.

4. **Comprehensive Services**: The Massachusetts Conference offers the following process to closing congregations as a way to assist congregations in the disposition of real estate, distribution of assets and satisfying legal requirements under Mass. law to legally dissolve the church's non-profit entity status:

   a. The church would establish a date for their final worship service

   b. The church would decide on its financial legacy—how it would like to have all remaining funds distributed.

      i) A memorandum of understanding is entered into which provides for the ultimate distribution of net proceeds (proceeds after all costs of maintaining the building(s) until sale, real estate commissions, legal costs, associated administrative, and other direct costs) from the disposition of real estate and other church unrestricted funds.

      ii) If the anticipated final amount available for distribution is less than $100,000, 100% of the distribution must be received into one or more Conference funds.

      iii) If the anticipated final amount available for distribution is greater than $100,000, 75% of the distribution must be received into one or more Conference funds.

      iv) Other beneficiaries must meet the requirements of the Commonwealth of Massachusetts regarding religious purposes.

   c. An environmental assessment would be performed on any real estate involved to assure the marketability of the property.

d. The church would amend its by-law, effective as of the date of the final worship service to provide:

    i) The form of organization would be changed from a membership-based organization to a board of directors without members.

    ii) The new board of directors would be selected by the Board of Directors of the Conference. It would include a person representing the Association the church belongs to.

    iiii) The new Board of Directors would take all steps necessary to dispose of real and other property, pay any remaining debts and obligations, and undertake the necessary legal process to dissolve the organization and distribute remaining assets as provided for in paragraph (b) and as approved by the Attorney General's Office and the Supreme Judicial Court of the Commonwealth of Massachusetts.

Additional Resources

FOR ADDITIONAL READING BY the author on church downsizing, merger, and closure, please visit her blog, "From Death to Life," which is written to accompany this book. It can be found at http://freelancepastor.wordpress.com, and on *The Christian Century Blogs Network*.

BOOKS

Ackerman, John, and Alice Mann. *Listening to God: Spiritual Formation in Congregations*. Herndon, VA: Alban Institute, 2001.

Bush, Peter. *In Dying We Are Born: The Challenge and the Hope for Congregations*. Herndon, VA: Alban Institute, 2008.

Claiborne, Shane. *The Irresistible Revolution*. Grand Rapids, MI: Zondervan, 2006.

Freidman, Edwin H. *A Failure of Nerve: Leadership in the Age of the Quick Fix*. New York: Seabury Books, 2007.

Gifford, Mary Louise. *The Turnaround Church*. Herndon, VA: Alban Institute, 2009.

Hammond, Sue Annis. *The Thin Book of Appreciative Inquiry*. Bend, OR: Thin Book Publishing Co., 1996.

Harder, Cameron. *Discovering the Other: Asset-Based Approaches for Building Community Together*. Herndon, VA: Alban Institute, 2013.

Hilliard, Linda M., and Gretchen J. Switzer. *Finishing with Grace*. Self-published, 2010.

LaRochelle, Robert. *Part Time Pastor, Full Time Church*. Cleveland, OH: Pilgrim Press, 2010.

MacFayden, Kenneth J. *Strategic Leadership for a Change*. Herndon, VA: Alban Institute, 2009.

Morris, Danny E., and Charles M. Olsen. *Discerning God's Will Together.* Nashville, TN: Upper Room, 1997.

Snow, Luther K. *The Power of Asset Mapping: How Your Congregation Can Act on Its Gifts.* Herndon, VA: Alban Institute, 2004.

Willis, Steve. *Imagining the Small Church.* Herndon, VA: Alban Institute, 2012.

ONLINE RESOURCES

Duggan, Joseph. *Congregational Seasons: A Resource for Transitions.* http://congregationalseasons.blogspot.com/.

Mann, Alice. "The Smaller Congregation—Pathways in Challenging Times." http://www.alban.org/uploadedFiles/Alban/Bookstore/Books/SmallerCongregationChallengingTimes.pdf.

CONSULTING ORGANIZATIONS

The Alban Institute
> http://www.alban.org.
> Publishing, workshops, and coaching on church leadership issues offered to an ecumenical audience.

Church Collaboration: How Congregations Can Work Together for Mission
> http://www.churchcollaboration.com/default.html.
> Minneapolis, Minnesota–based coaching and consulting.

Church Innovations
> http://www.churchinnovations.org.
> Minneapolis, Minnesota–based consulting services.

The Center for Parish Development
> http://www.missionalchurch.org.
> Consulting and online education based in Palatine, Illinois.

The Center for Progressive Renewal
> http://www.progressiverenewal.org.
> Web-based leadership training and workshops on new church development and vitality.

Additional Resources

The Columbia Partnership
> http://www.thecolumbiapartnership.org.
> Coaching, consulting, and web-based education based in Columbia, South Carolina.

New Beginnings
> http://www.hopepmt.org/transform/new-beginnings/about-new -beginnings/
> A Disciples of Christ organization offering churches and judicatories trained, on-site consultants for vitality and viability assessment, based in Indianapolis, Indiana.

Mission Insight
> http://www.missioninsite.com
> Offers demographic data about your geographical region, including the religious and cultural practices of your neighbors. They can also help churches assess strengths and weaknesses based on input you provide.

Partners for Sacred Places
> http://www.sacredplaces.org/
> A Philadelphia, Pennsylvania–based nonprofit organization that offers consulting services to help churches build partnerships with other nonprofits, train leaders for capital campaigns, and preserve historic church buildings.

Sand-bur Church Consulting
> http://www.sandburconsulting.com
> Wisconsin-based consulting and coaching for UCC and PCUSA churches.

CHURCH DATA

Pew Forum on Religion and Public Life. Pew Research Center (October 9, 2012). http://www.pewforum.org/about/.

Roozen, David. *Faith Communities Today.* "American Congregations 2008." Hartford, CT: Hartford Institute for Religion Research, 2009. http://faithcommunitiestoday.org/sites/faithcommunitiestoday.org/files/American_Congregations_2008.pdf.

OTHER

Bauman, Kevin. Small Churches
http://www.kevinbauman.com/projects/small_churches
A poignant photographic journal of abandoned storefront churches in Detroit.

Bibliography

All Web sites listed in this book were accessible as of July 24, 2013.

2X2 Virtual Church. "SEPA/Redeemer." No pages. Online: http://2x2virtualchurch.com/separedeemer/.

Association of Religious Data Archives. No pages. Online: http://www.thearda.com.

Bullard, George. "Is Attendance in Your Congregation Declining? Think Again." *George Bullard Journal* (October 4, 2012). No pages. Online: http://www.bullard journal.org.

———. "Mission Banality Revisited." *George Bullard Journal* (May 13, 2013). No pages. Online: http://www.bullardjournal.org.

"PCUSA Membership Drop in 2012." *Christian Century* 130, No. 13 (June 26, 2013). Online http://www.christiancentury.org/article/2013-06/pcusa-membership-drop-2012-exceeds-2011-slide

Christian Church (Disciples of Christ). "About New Beginnings." No pages. Online: http://www.hopepmt.org/transform/new-beginnings/about-new-beginnings/.

Dunigan, Erin. "A Change of Scenery." *Presbyterian News Service* (April 3, 2012). No pages. Online: http://www.pcusa.org/news/2012/4/3/change-scenery/.

"Earthly Concerns." *The Economist* (August 18, 2012). No pages. Online: http://www.economist.com/node/21560536.

Frykholm, Amy, and Robert Wuthnow. "Loose Connections." *The Christian Century* (May 16, 2011). No pages. Online: http://www.christiancentury.org/article/2011-05/loose-connections.

Gaede, Beth Ann. *Ending with Hope.* Herndon, VA: Alban, 2002.

Hamman, Jaco. *When Steeples Cry.* Cleveland, OH: Pilgrim Press, 2005.

Heifetz, Ron, and Martin Linsky. *Leadership on the Line.* Boston, MA: Harvard Business School Press, 2002.

Hospice Foundation of America. "Grief." No pages. Online: http://www.hospicefoundation.org/grief.

Hughes, Philip J. "Lay Leadership in Sparsely Populated Rural Australia." Abstract (2010). Edith Cowan University. No pages. Online: http://ro.ecu.edu.au/ecuworks/6391/.

Jenks, Philip E. "National Council of Churches 2009 Yearbook." National Council of Churches (February 23, 2009). Online: http://www.ncccusa.org/news/090130year book1.html.

Kids Count Data Center. No pages. Online: http://datacenter.kidscount.org/data/tables/106-children-in-single-parent-families?loc=1&loct=2#detailed/1/any/false/867,133,38,35,18/any/429,430.

Kimura, Greg. *Cargo.* Self-published, 2012.

King, David. "Smaller for a Purpose." *Sandbur Consulting* (May 4, 2012). No pages. Online: http://sandburconsulting.com/wordpress/.

Kosmin, Barry A., and Ariela Keysar. "American Religion Identification Survey (ARIS), 2008. Trinity College. No pages. Online: Bibliography.

Kramer, Don. "To the Point." *Non-Profit Issues.* No pages. Online: http://www.nonprofit issues.com/public/features/point/250.html.

Light, Joe. "Joblessness Hits the Pulpit." *The Wall Street Journal* (May 17, 2010). Online: http://online.wsj.com/article/SB10001424052748703648304575212001278867126 .html.

Lonie, William. "The History of Melrose." Melrose, Scotland. No pages. Online: http: //www.melrose.bordernet.co.uk/mha/5/mailros.html.

Lonie, William. "Melrose Abbey and the Heart of the Bruce." *Melrose Historical Association,* Bulletin No. 5. Online: http://www.melrose.bordernet.co.uk/history.

Maciejewski, Paul K., et al. "An Empirical Examination of the Stage Theory of Grief." Abstract. *Journal of the American Medical Association* 297, No. 7 (February 21, 2007). No pages. Online: http://jama.jamanetwork.com/article.aspx?articleid=205661.

Mann, Alice. *Can Our Church Live?* Herndon, VA: Alban, 2000.

McRay, Greg. "Are You Misappropriating Your Nonprofit's Funds?" *The Foundation Group* (December 16, 2009). No pages. Online: http://www.501c3.org/blog /misappropriating-nonprofit-funds/.

Moore, Janet. "Three Churches Go Condo." *Minneapolis Star Tribune* (February 24, 2012). Online: http://www.startribune.com/business/140385793.html.

"Neighborhood Memory Café Toolkit." *Third Age Services.* No pages. Online: http: //thirdageservices.com/MemoryCafe.html.

New Revised Standard Version Bible. New York: Oxford University Press, 1962.

Newport, Frank. "Americans' Church Attendance Inches Up." *Gallup* (June 25, 2010). No pages. Online: http://www.gallup.com/poll/141044/americans-church-attendance -inches-2010.aspx.

Nixon, Paul. *I Refuse to Lead a Dying Church.* Cleveland, OH: Pilgrim Press, 2006.

"Partners for Sacred Places." No pages. Online: http://www.sacredplaces.org/.

The Presbyterian Church (U.S.A.). *The Book of Order: The Constitution of the Presbyterian Church (U.S.A.), Part 2,* 2005–2007. Louisville, KY: Office of the General Assembly.

Putnam, Robert. *Bowling Alone.* New York: Simon & Schuster, 2000.

Rabinowitz, Phil. "Understanding and Writing Contracts and Memoranda of Agreement." *The Community Tool Box* (2013). No pages. Online: http://ctb.ku.edu/en /tablecontents/sub_section_main_1873.aspx.

Raymond, David. "Blending by Continuation Merger." *Church Collaboration.* No pages. Online: http://www.churchcollaboration.com/.

Robertson, Russell G. Robertson, and Marcos Montagnini. "Geriatric Failure to Thrive." *American Family Physician* (July 15, 2004). No pages. Online: http://geriatrics .uthscsa.edu/reading%20resources/FailureToThrive.pdf.

Robinson, Anthony B. *Changing the Conversation.* Grand Rapids, MI: Wm. B. Eerdmans, 2008.

Santa Cruz, Nicole. "O.C. Catholic Diocese to Buy Bankrupt Crystal Cathedral." *Los Angeles Times* (November 18, 2011). Online: http://articles.latimes.com/2011/nov/18 /local/la-me-crystal-cathedral-20111118.

Schlumpf, Heidi. "An Unholy Mess." *National Catholic Reporter* (August 17, 2012). No pages. Online: http://ncronline.org/blogs/ncr-today/unholy-mess.

Shanks, Carol. *Choosing to Be a What If Church.* Self-published, 2011.

Smietana, Bob. "Statistical Illusion." *Christianity Today* (April 1, 2006). Online: http://www.christianitytoday.com/ct/2006/april/32.85.html.

Steinke, Peter. *Congregational Leadership in Anxious Times.* Herndon, VA: Alban, 2006.

Sullivan, Louis H. "The Tall Office Building Artistically Considered." *Lippincott's Magazine* (March 1896). Online: http://www.gwu.edu/~art/Temporary_SL/177/pdfs/Sullivan_Tall.pdf.

Tomberlin, Jim, and Warren Bird. *Better Together.* San Francisco: Jossey-Bass, 2012.

Toossi, Miltra. "A Century of Change." *Monthly Labor Review* (May, 2002). No pages. Online: http://www.bls.gov/opub/mlr/2002/05/art2full.pdf.

Unitarian Universalist Association of Congregations. "Dissolution Clause: Writing Congregational Bylaws" (February 7, 2013). No pages. Online: http://www.uua.org/governance/bylaws/48001.shtml.

United Church of Christ. "2011 Annual Report." Online: http://uccfiles.com/pdf/ar2011.pdf.

United Methodist Church. *The Book of Discipline of the United Methodist Church.* Nashville, TN: United Methodist Publishing House, 2008.

Weldon, Michael. *A Struggle for Holy Ground.* Collegeville, MN: Liturgical Press, 2004.

Youngs, Sharon. "Stated Clerk Releases PC (USA) 2009 Statistics." *Presbyterian News Service* (July 1, 2010). No pages. Online: http://www.pcusa.org/news/2010/7/1/stated-clerk-releases-pcusa-2009-statistics/.

CPSIA information can be obtained
at www.ICGtesting.com
Printed in the USA
LVHW041744221019
634994LV00037B/2271/P